SCENE OF THE CRIME
A Writer's Guide to
Crime-Scene Investigations

by
Anne Wingate, Ph.D.

Writer's Digest Books

Cincinnati, Ohio

96   95   94   93   5   4   3

Library of Congress Cataloging-in-Publication Data

Wingate, Anne.
     Scene of the crime : a writer's guide to crime-scene investigations / by Anne
Wingate.
          p.   cm.
     Includes bibliographical references and index.
     ISBN 0-89879-518-4
     1. Criminal investigation—Handbooks, manuals, etc. 2. Criminal investiga-
tion—United States—Handbooks, manuals, etc. I. Title.
HV8073.W527   1992
363.2'5'02483—dc20   92-15730
                                                                         CIP

Edited by Charles Clark
Cover illustration by Chris Spollen

To Paul and Shirley Smith
Thanks

Acknowledgments

No book can be written without the help of many people. In working on this one, I have received much assistance from many people, some of whom were dead long before I even thought of this book.

Thanks go to —

Clinton "Doc" Luther and Wayne Posey of the Albany, Georgia, Police Department, for not chasing away a reporter who was hanging around altogether too often and Luther again for teaching me so much and being such a terrific mentor, boss and partner; Chief Ed Friend, who took a chance on creating a new secretarial position and hiring an ex-reporter to fill it; Chief Leslie Summerford, for rehiring me as a police officer and assigning me exactly where I wanted to be assigned; Chief Norman Denney, then Chief of Detectives, for his patience; and all the men and women of the Albany Police Department and the Plano Police Department for being such wonderful friends and coworkers.

Dear friends in the FBI, the Secret Service and the Postal Inspection Service who, for official policy reasons, must not be named herein. They know who they are.

Elizabeth Linington (pen names: Dell Shannon and Lesley Egan) for her friendship to me and her mentorship as I learned inch-by-inch how to write fiction, and the executors of her estate, who ensured that I could afford to purchase her professional library and add it to my own. (Elizabeth worried that her library would be neglected and scattered after her death, and I promised her I would use it and take care of it.) I think she would be pleased to see how useful it continues to be.

My agent, Joshua Bilmes of the Scott Meredith Agency, who does not hesitate to return a proposal to me if he thinks it needs to be rewritten, and who makes useful suggestions and comes up with useful ideas.

Editor Bill Brohaugh of Writer's Digest Books, who saw much more potential in the original proposal for this book than I did, and who has carefully guided its writing.

Jim Gocke at Sirchie Finger Print Laboratories, Inc., for his permission to reprint several fine charts from Sirchie's advertising material.

My former student at the University of Utah, Joel Grose, for deciding to write a research paper on a topic I needed to look up, and for allowing me to quote from his work.

The officers of the Salt Lake City Police Department Identification Section, especially Lynn Bergen, for updating me on changes since I left the fingerprint field and explaining AFIS so clearly to me.

The men and women of the FBI Latent Fingerprint Section and the Utah State Crime Lab, who have been extremely patient with answering questions.

Mark McComb, of Point Blank Firearms in Utah, for spending hours looking up material I had no access to.

The librarians at every library I've ever used, especially Judith Ireland and David Miles of the Rose Park Branch of the Salt Lake City Library, without whose help I would be dead in the water.

My editor, Charles Clark, for the many useful suggestions he has made and the additional information he has provided.

My writing students at the Writer's Digest School and the University of Utah, for coming up with thoughtful questions and suggestions.

My children and stepchildren, especially Alicia, for doing a lot of dishwashing and snow shoveling while Mom was glued to the computer. (No, I do not think it is rude to call my stepchildren stepchildren. They and their mother, my dear friend Naomi, would rightly be offended if I tried to usurp Naomi's position.)

Alice Schiesswohl and the many other people, especially my sons-in-law Jeff Adams and Joe Stencel, who help to provide me encouragement, friendship and transportation when I'm stuck.

And most especially my husband, T. Russell Wingate, who should be listed as coauthor on most of my books.

Any errors are my own, and come from misunderstanding material that was in front of me. But as to differences in interpretation, or reporting case histories, I can only reply that each of us sees the world from a different point of view; I see it from mine. If someone else disagrees, we may both be right.

Table of Contents

8 **The Autopsy and After**   *160*

How an autopsy is performed, what information it can yield, and how that information is used in criminal investigations.

9 **Inside the Crime Lab**   *182*

Functions, procedures and uses of the crime lab in analyzing many types of evidence.

10 **The Unofficial Investigator**   *205*

How private detectives, reporters and amateur sleuths overcome obstacles that official investigators don't face.

Introduction

This is the safe that Jack cracked.

This is the prybar that cracked the safe that Jack cracked.

This is the fingerprint left on the prybar that cracked the safe that Jack cracked.

This is the powder that showed the fingerprint left on the prybar that cracked the safe that Jack cracked.

This is the photo made of the powder that showed the fingerprint left on the prybar that cracked the safe that Jack cracked.

This is the inked print that matched the photo made of the powder that showed the fingerprint left on the prybar that cracked the safe that Jack cracked.

This is the jury that saw the inked print that matched the photo made of the powder that showed the fingerprint left on the prybar that cracked the safe that Jack cracked.

This is the "Guilty!" said by the jury that saw the inked print that matched the photo made of the powder that showed the fingerprint left on the prybar that cracked the safe that Jack cracked.

In real life, we wish it were always that simple.

Sometimes it is. Once I went to a service station burglary. Recognizing the fingerprint (Yes, I know this is theoretically impossible, but I can't help that—sometimes I did it anyway.) on the broken glass as that of a known burglar and forger who had fled town six months before, I asked the owner if he had any checks missing. He told me he didn't.

All too well acquainted with the habits of that particular burglar, I said, "I'm sure you do. Look in the very back of the checkbook."

He did, and to his surprise—but not mine—the last few checks had been torn out. "Seventy-four to detective bureau," I said into my radio. "So-and-so is back in town."

"Thank you," replied Detective Johnny Patton. "En route."

As I went on to other calls, Detectives Patton and Bob Prickett (Yes, these are their real names; I always enjoyed working with them.) hauled the surprised burglar out of his girlfriend's bed, and jailed him before I got back to the police station.

It isn't usually that easy or that fast—and even when it is, it's easy only because all the homework has been done and all the investigators involved know what they're doing.

In fiction, we want it to be complicated. But no matter how complicated it is, accuracy is important. We're not talking about avoiding that combination of sheer lunacy and total laziness that sometimes turns up in pulp fiction, such as that exhibited by the author who had a security guard in an intelligence agency carrying a *cocked revolver inside* his jumpsuit. Unless the guard had a real yen to sing soprano, he wouldn't.

No, we're talking about the mysteries that could be good and just miss because of inaccuracies. One such mystery — by a brilliant writer — was ruined for me because the author assumed identical triplets would have identical fingerprints. They don't; no identical siblings have identical fingerprints. Another book, by an even more brilliant writer, was similarly ruined because, in the second chapter, the author described a brain as ruby red. I spent the rest of the book waiting expectantly for some exotic poison that would have turned the brain ruby red. There wasn't one. It turned out to be a simple bashing. Years later, I had a chance to meet that author. When I pointed out to him that the brain is light gray, bearing a distinct resemblance to lumpy oatmeal, he replied ruefully, "Now I know. But I didn't then."

However, that same author had redeemed himself, in my eyes, by writing absolutely the most precise and accurate description of the search for latent fingerprints at a crime scene that I had ever read in any book including my own, and I'm a certified latent fingerprint examiner. I asked him how he'd managed that, and he told me he'd spent two weeks following a fingerprint unit of the New York City Police Department everywhere they went, and asking every question he could think of.

Most of us have neither the time nor the resources to make that kind of an odyssey. We want our work, whether we're writing fictional mysteries or true crime articles or books, to be as accurate as possible. But for most of us, there's no way to know how a crime scene is *really* worked or what *really* happens at the crime lab. We depend on what we read in magazines or glean from books written for specialists.

I spent five and a half years as a police officer attached to the Major Crime Scene Unit in Albany, Georgia (which was then listed as the smallest Standard Metropolitan Area in the United States), and another year as head of the Identification and Crime Scene Unit in Plano, the "Silicon Valley" of Texas. Since then, I've made every effort to keep up with new processes and methods as they have been developed. And here's an example of how things change: When I first began fingerprint work, it was impossible to get the fingerprints of an assailant from the skin of a victim. By the time I left, less than ten years later, there were three methods for doing just that, and I had the equipment for two of them.

At the time I left police work, about twelve years ago, the only way to "search a latent" — that is, compare an unknown latent fingerprint from a crime scene to fingerprints of known criminals, when no suspect has been developed otherwise — was manually. In even a small town, that could take months or even years. I once cleared a robbery exactly one year after it took place, and the month Captain "Doc" Luther and I cleared twenty-four cases, each involving a different criminal, by fingerprints alone, we felt like dancing in the streets. In those days, if the inked prints were filed anywhere other than in the police department that had collected the latent, almost certainly the criminal would never be identified by fingerprints alone. Now this work is done by computer. Local and state files can be searched in minutes, and the vast FBI fingerprint file can be searched in a matter of hours.

When I left police work, genetic fingerprinting did not exist. Now just about everybody has heard of it, and it's turning up in fiction as fast as it is in real life.

This book is as up to date as it can be, but in some areas it will be outdated before it is off the press. So use this as a starting point, and keep reading.

O N E
_____

WORKING THE CRIME SCENE

*A quality demanded at any price from the Investigating Officer is
absolute accuracy.*

> —Hans Gross,
> *Criminal Investigation*

Let's walk through a real crime. I've changed a few details, partly
for protection of those innocently involved, partly because the
crime, after all, was eighteen years ago, and I've forgotten this and
that. But with those exceptions, everything is as it was then—except,
you are there.

The Jackson Street Corpse

Saturday, August 17th. It is hot in the city, hot and so humid that
the air is not just sticky but almost dripping. It's rained every afternoon for a week, and everything is molding including the clothes
you're wearing.

Uniform division gets the call first. It's probably nothing. A
citizen has reported a bad smell and a lot of flies in a thick growth
of bamboo between two "shotgun" houses. You know the reason
for the nickname: These houses are laid out in straight-line fashion,

and they're so small that if you fire a shotgun through the front door of one of them, the shot pattern will just about fill the back wall.

Uniform division has no trouble finding the house. The officers are used to this address. Three middle-aged winos live together here, two sleeping in the double bed and one on the couch, and when they're not drinking, they're fighting with each other.

The call looks simple, at first. . . .

Who Gets the Call First?

In all but the very smallest jurisdictions, where there are no more than two or three police officers at the most, uniform division gets the call first. What happens then varies from jurisdiction to jurisdiction. Where I worked, if the crime was "heavy"—that is, if it was a serious crime, such as murder or armed robbery—detectives would be dispatched at the same time the uniform officers were dispatched, but would generally arrive later because detectives are not usually in the immediate area; the beat car is. Identification Section—sometimes called the Major Crime Scene Unit—would be requested by the first officers at the scene if photographs, fingerprinting or evidence collection was needed. But every jurisdiction has far fewer ident technicians than uniform officers or detectives, so depending on how busy ident is, ident might get there considerably later.

When the detectives arrive, the uniform officers back off. They may be asked to "control the scene"—that is, to keep unauthorized people out of the way; they may be asked to help with questioning and transporting witnesses. If there are many witnesses and the scene is somewhat chaotic, patrol officers may be called from other beats and the patrol sergeant will come to help direct crime-scene protection.

Detectives will question some witnesses at the scene and transport others to the police station to make formal, written statements.

But in a fairly large police department, ident section actually does the crime-scene work.

So for the time being, you—Detective N.E. Boddy—work in ident.

It looked simple, to start with.

But by the time you get there, an emergency medical technician is vomiting in his gas mask, and the coroner has just pronounced the victim dead from half a block away.

The victim might be one of the winos, but you can't tell by looking, not now. His own mother wouldn't recognize him now.

After death, and after something—you don't yet know what—that left the body curiously flattened, he was bent double and wrapped in quilts loosely wired around him with straightened metal coat hangers. After semiconcealing the unwieldy bundle in the bamboo thicket, the culprit—henceforth to be called the "perp" (police slang for "perpetrator")—laid a sheet of plyboard over the bundle.

But the moisture and the flies had no trouble getting into the coverings, and the body has been dead for at least a week. It's semidecayed, seething with writhing white footballs composed of thousands of maggots.

Somebody has gone to get a search warrant, to allow you inside the house where the death—natural, suicide or homicide, but the disposition of the body tells you which is most likely—almost certainly occurred.

The case is all yours.

Enjoy.

When Do You Need a Search Warrant?

You need a search warrant any time the person in control of the location—not necessarily the owner—is either unable or unwilling to sign a consent-to-search form.

At the time this case was really worked, you did not need a search warrant to work a crime scene. We just went in and set to work. But as a result of more recent Supreme Court decisions, you now do need a search warrant in such situations.

If the premises are rented, "the person in control of the location" is the renter, rather than the owner, because the owner has in effect rented the control of the location to the renter. If husband and wife together rent or own a house and the wife signs a consent-to-search form, police may not search the workshop which is used only by her husband unless he also signs, because he is in control of that location. Similarly, the husband may not give police consent to search the wife's sewing room.

Under what circumstances may a search warrant be issued? Read the U.S. Constitution. The rules are spelled out in careful detail. We'll discuss them after you've had time to think about them a little.

Learn the Givens, Then Break the Rules

Do not try to break the rules spelled out in the U.S. Constitution.

Given Number One: The ideal situation is what you never have.

Given Number Two: Whatever you didn't write down is the first thing the defense attorney is going to ask you.

Given Number Three: The least competent person on the police department is always the first on the scene; hence, witnesses' names will be omitted or recorded incorrectly unless you do it yourself. If not carefully watched, s/he will—heedless of locations, heedless of fingerprints—proudly collect and bring to you the shotgun which was fired at your fellow officer, which half the department has been out here looking for.

I swear. It happened to me. And I don't think the turkey ever did figure out why his sergeant, his lieutenant, my captain and I all began screaming at him. I had him in mind when I created the character of Patrolman Danny Shea in my first Deb Ralston novel, *Too Sane a Murder.*

WHAT DO YOU DO FIRST?

Rule #1: Don't touch anything.
Rule #2: Don't touch anything.
Rule #3: Don't touch anything.
Rule #4: Don't touch anything.
Rule #5: Don't touch anything.

Unless there is an injured person who must be helped and transported at once. In that case, assist the victim as much as you can until the medical team arrives; remember as much as you can; make notes if you are not needed for the first-aid effort; *get out of the way* if necessary; and after the ambulance has departed, do what you can with what's left.

The Deathbed Statement

This is as good a place as any to mention the deathbed statement. Under normal situations, no person may testify as to what any person other than the defendant said to him or in his hearing, because the law assumes that the person who said whatever it was is perfectly capable of coming into court and testifying. The one exception is the deathbed statement, and the rules that define it—carried over from English common law—are pretty specific:

1. The person making the deathbed statement must know s/he is dying.
2. The person must really die.

In that one situation, what would otherwise be considered hearsay testimony and, hence, be inadmissible, becomes admissible. The legal presumption is that a person who knows s/he is dying has no reason to lie.

Getting a deathbed statement is likely to feel pretty brutal to the officer asking for it, and to witnesses, to say nothing of the way it must feel to the dying person. The conversation would go something like this:

Officer:	You understand that you're dying?
Victim:	Uh-huh.
Officer:	Who shot you?
Victim:	My wife.
Officer:	Why'd she want to do that?
Victim:	Said I was messin' around. . . .

(Victim dies.)

The officer may now testify as to what the victim said.

Rule # 6: Write everything down.
Rule # 7: Write everything down.
Rule # 8: Write everything down.
Rule # 9: Write everything down.
Rule #10: Write everything down.

Everything means everything. What time of day is it? What day of the week? What is the outside temperature? What are the weather conditions otherwise? Which other officers are present?

What is the building made of? How many windows and doors does it have on the front? What color clothes is the victim wearing? Is the victim lying face up or face down? Was the door open or closed?

I'm serious—I saw a case lost in court once because two officers who arrived at the scene together could not agree on the position of a car door. One told the defense attorney a car door was open; the other said it was closed. Although the position of the car door was absolutely immaterial in terms of whether the defendant was guilty, the defense attorney managed to convince the jury that if the officers could not agree on whether the door was open or shut, they obviously could not be trusted on anything else.

Rule #11: Isolate the witnesses.

Isolate means isolate. Keep them apart. Don't let them talk with one another. If they discuss the crime before they've made their formal statements, they'll begin to conflate stories and agree on details—and they might not agree correctly. It will always be the person with the strongest personality, not the person who is the best observer, who will impose his/her opinions on everybody else. (This knowledge, of course, can make a terrific red herring—or yellow herring, if you prefer—in your story.)

Personally, I wouldn't hang a mad dog on the basis of eyewitness testimony. Psychologists are agreeing more and more on what good police officers knew all along: Eyewitness testimony is the next worse thing to worthless. Memory is funny. It plays tricks on people. It wants very much to cooperate, so it thinks up things that might have been useful if they had actually happened the way the witness remembers them as having happened.

Rule #12: Define the scene.

The crime scene is what you have to protect. But just how large an expanse does the crime scene cover? It may be no more than one small part of one small room; it may be an entire house; it may be the interior of an automobile, or an entire city block or—as in one case I was involved with—a whole swamp.

Be sure that whoever's protecting the scene protects it from everybody. Whether it is a reporter who handles the bank door the robber handled on the way out before you've had a chance to finger-print it, or the chief of police who does it, the evidence is just as demolished. An adequately protected scene can produce wonderful results.

Perjury Wholesale

In one case, the robbery of a small mom-and-pop grocery store and the shooting (fortunately not fatal) of its owner, the store was in the process of closing when the robber walked in. The store owner had just finished wiping down the meat counter. The robber put his entire hand flat on the meat counter—and the victim, despite his serious injury, managed to convey that information to the first police officer on the scene before the ambulance departed.

The D.A. did not present the fingerprint evidence in his original case. The defense produced six witnesses who claimed the defendant had been at a football game at the time of the robbery. The prosecution produced, as rebuttal, the fingerprint evidence. The jury convicted. And the six alibi witnesses were arrested in *the courtroom* and charged with perjury. Some of us enjoyed that case. The defendant and his friends did not.

Too Many People at the Scene

Every police officer knows these rules. Every private investigator should know them. Nonetheless, they're more often honored in the breach than in the observance. If you read *Helter Skelter*, you know that investigation was complicated by the fact that someone— nobody ever confessed—kicked a weapon under the couch. In a much more ordinary case, the murder of a prostitute in a small town in south Georgia, I saw twenty-five police officers, only one of whom had any business there, crowded into one small motel room.

What your fictional detective does is your business, and you'll decide that on the basis of the personality of the character and the needs of the plot. You may well want to let your detective—or your detective's rival—do anything or everything I say *not* to do, for the purpose of plot complications or red herrings. But for now, assume that you are your fictional detective. Here's what you should do:

Don't Touch Anything

In real life, officers are (or should be) instructed to put their hands in their pockets or clasp them behind their backs, while they do their initial walk-through. Then they should begin to make notes of what is significant, remembering that they don't know what is significant until the case is concluded. Here are some apparently unimportant things that in my experience later proved to be extremely significant:

- Black candles on the fireplace mantel — and if the spell to lure your enemy to his destruction doesn't work, you can always resort to the telephone.

- The color of slacks a woman was wearing. We thought at first it was natural death. It wasn't. And six months later a fifteen-year-old boy confessed to strangling "an old lady in green pants." Fortunately one detective had thought to note the color of slacks the woman had on. I hadn't. I should have.

- A pair of pantyhose on the dresser in the motel room, and the package they came out of. We assumed the victim — who apparently was deliberately drowned in the toilet — had opened the package to put the stockings on. In fact, the perp had opened the package and used the stockings to strangle the victim, stopping up the toilet and putting the victim in head-first as an afterthought after returning the stockings to the dresser. By the time we learned that, the pantyhose and the package were in the county landfill.

- The chemical composition of what appeared to be the last in a series of blood puddles, where an injured murderer had repeatedly paused to get his breath. It turned out to be red brake fluid. We'd lost the trail half a block back.

Officers are instructed not to remove anything from the scene, no matter how insignificant it may appear, without properly collecting it. If an investigating officer hadn't decided to flush an upstairs toilet that had a cigarette floating in it, Sam Sheppard might never have been convicted of murder. And, of course, no one should ever add anything to the scene. An investigator's own cigarette butts may confuse the situation badly. In one rape murder, the medical examiner found a combination of spittle and the chewed end of a toothpick in the pubic hair of the victim. It looked significant — until one of the investigating officers confessed that he did the spitting, trying to keep from vomiting and not aiming to hit where he did.

Who Was Sam Sheppard?

He was the man on whom the television series *The Fugitive*, my novel *The Eye of Anna*, and probably many other novels, were loosely based.

It happened in the early 1950s in a suburb of Cleveland, Ohio. Sheppard's wife Marilyn was bludgeoned to death during the night. According to the prosecution, Sheppard — an osteopath — was guilty. According to the defense, Sheppard was asleep in a downstairs room at the time of the event; he awoke to hear his wife's screams; when he tried to run upstairs to her aid, he was knocked unconscious by a bushy-haired stranger.

Sheppard was convicted and served ten years in prison but was finally released partly as a result of the aid of Erle Stanley Gardner and his "Court of Last Resort," a foundation Gardner established to aid people who appeared to have been unjustly convicted of major crimes. Books have been written arguing for Sheppard's innocence; books have been written arguing for Sheppard's guilt.

The only thing that is absolutely certain is that the crime-scene investigation was hideously botched. For one thing, when the first officers arrived at the scene, there was a cigarette floating in an upstairs bathroom adjoining the bedroom where Mrs. Sheppard was killed. Neither Dr. Sheppard nor Mrs. Sheppard smoked.

Somebody flushed the cigarette, and Sam Sheppard did ten years.

Was he guilty?

Danged if I know. But I do know there was a reasonable doubt, which means he shouldn't have been convicted.

If the crime scene had been done right, there might never have been a question — whichever side was right.

Notes. Sketches. Measurements, triangulated from two fixed points so that the exact spot can always be found again. Photographs, preferably color. And never make assumptions. The victim is lying in a pool of what appears to be blood. Sure, you know it's blood, I know it's blood, everybody knows it's blood — but what if your report said it was blood and it turned out to be red paint, or catsup, or — as in the situation above — brake fluid. So let the lab say what it is.

The victim *appeared* to have been shot, or drowned, or whatever. But let the medical examiner (sometimes referred to as the ME) decide the actual cause of death, or you may find yourself — as I once was — on the receiving end of a telephone call that includes a lot of undeleted expletives. "What do you mean, natural death? That woman died of a broken neck!"

It was at least mildly funny when I adapted it fifteen years later to use in a novel. It was a lot less amusing when it was the real ME screaming at me, even though I had not been involved in the initial investigation—which is just as well, because I, too, would almost certainly have assumed it was natural death. After all, isn't it logical to assume that a woman known to have severe heart trouble, found lying dead on her back in her nightgown in a neatly made bed inside her locked house, died naturally? We thought so, anyway.

Medical Examiner or Coroner?

You'll have to find out what your jurisdiction has.

The coroner system is based, like so many other things, on English common law. The coroner may be elected; s/he may be totally unqualified, or may be qualified only as a funeral director and undertaker. The coroner may be appointed, in which case s/he usually has some medical qualifications.

The medical examiner is almost always appointed, and s/he almost always has some medical qualifications; often s/he is a board-certified pathologist.

In many jurisdictions that by law—often as a result of the state constitution—have an elected (and often unqualified) coroner, a coroner system and a medical examiner system exist side by side. Such a situation is ideal if the coroner and medical examiner work together; it is a nightmare if they fight each other.

A small town may have no medical examiner at all, or may have a multi-county arrangement with one medical examiner serving several small towns. A very large city, on the other hand, will probably have a team of coroners and assistant coroners, or medical examiners and assistant medical examiners. Thomas Noguchi, former deputy coroner of the city of Los Angeles, has written two extremely interesting books showing how the system works.

But now, back to our corpse. You don't know what he died of. Nobody does, yet. All you know is that he's dead, and the way the body was hidden strongly suggests murder.

This time, you won't have any trouble at all with extra people at the crime scene. Nobody wants anywhere near this one. You don't either, but you're stuck with it.

You can wear a gas mask, which is what the ME will do, later, when he's doing the postmortem examination. Or you can wear a floater mask, a modified gas mask designed only to filter out bad smells. But if you're like me—a gas mask doesn't fit around your glasses, and a floater mask fogs them so badly that you can't see— you just go in. This makes you look very macho, even if you do happen to be a five-foot-tall grandmother.

Here's the secret—and let's not tell it to those standing at a distance watching and admiring you. If you stay in a bad odor about three minutes, your olfactory nerves go numb and you can no longer smell the odor. If you keep rushing out to get breaths of fresh air, every time you go back in it's just as bad as it was the first time. That's why I sat on the bumper of the car containing the late—the very, *very* late—Oscar (fake name, of course, and we'll get to this case in chapter five), while Georgia Bureau of Investigation agents were running in and out turning green and arguing frantically about towing the car to Americus with the body still in it, which of course would not have solved the problem of which one of them was *not* going to open the car door and take photographs.

I'm the one who took the photographs, surrendering my own copies years later to an FBI agent who wanted them to illustrate one of his lectures.

Dividing the Work

Now, who does what? If your detective is a small-town cop, s/he's going to do it all. In a larger city, most of the crime-scene work will be done by people who may be called the Identification Section, the Mobile Crime Scene Unit, or (in most of Britain) the Scene-of-Crimes officer. If you're writing about a real department, call and find out. They'll be glad to tell you, and will probably give you a tour of the section in the bargain.

For that matter, they'll give you such a tour even if you're creating a fictitious city. The Galveston Police Department was extraordinarily hospitable when I was doing the research for the first of my Mark Shigata novels, set in a nonexistent town in Galveston County.

But for the purposes of this book, let's assume that you (remember, you're a fictional detective right now) are a small-town cop. You get to do it all—but you're smart, well trained and well read, so you can handle it.

Back to the Jackson Street Corpse.

I don't have access to my original notes, sketches and reports, and after so many years, my memory is a little shaky. But that's OK, because we're—at least in a way—making this up as we go along, as I'll be doing with other cases in order to make my point in the most effective way.

You've walked through the scene. The unfortunate EMT is scrubbing the inside of his gas mask at a fire hydrant somebody turned on for him; the coroner has finished pronouncing the victim dead and is now cracking jokes with the other EMTs at a safe distance from the smell. You and another detective are hard at work.

And where do you begin?

What Do You Do—In Order?

1. Walk through the scene with your hands behind your back.
2. Take all your initial photographs.
3. Take any necessary close-up photos of the corpse, and mark the location of the corpse—with chalk inside, with rope outside—for future reference.
4. Let the corpse be removed *if* removing it won't interfere with anything you still have to do. This has to be decided on a case-by-case basis. If it would interfere, then wait until you can let it be removed. Someone—an ident officer if you have enough, otherwise a detective or a designated uniformed officer—should accompany the body to the hospital or morgue, to take any additional necessary photographs and take possession of the clothing.
5. Take measurements and draw initial rough sketches of the scene.
6. Fingerprint anything that is going to be fingerprinted at the scene.
7. Collect whatever evidence must be collected at the scene.
8. If possible, seal the scene, in case you need to return.
9. At all steps, keep very careful notes.
10. When the autopsy is scheduled, an ident officer should wit-

ness the autopsy in order to take immediate note of any additional information, and to take possession of the slug if any.

11. How long does it take? This is something that cannot, in justice to the victim and to the person who will ultimately be accused, be rushed. It takes as long as it takes. I've known crime-scene searches to take as short a time as fifteen minutes, as long a time as four days. Some—such as the Manson family's crime scenes, the Marilyn Sheppard crime scene—should have taken longer than they did.

12. Keep very detailed notes, and make supplementary reports as soon as possible. Remember that if anything happened to you—and in this business it could—somebody else might have to work from your notes and reports. I learned my lesson on that the day I rolled my car on the way back from a baseball game in Atlanta, with my report on a major murder not yet written and all my partner's and my notes on the crime scene in my purse. Fortunately nobody was injured and the notes remained intact.

13. Wash your hair before you go home. You don't really want to sit down to dinner smelling like *that*, do you? If you keep shampoo and a couple of towels in the locker room or (if you're a woman and they haven't set up a women's locker room yet) in the darkroom, it's easy enough to do. Lemon-scented shampoo helps. The smell gets into the hollow center of your hair shafts and into your sinuses, and it stays there. I never did figure out what to do about the sinuses. Eating hot horseradish or salsa followed by strong peppermints helps some.

Photographing the Scene

This time we can't let the corpse be moved yet—not that anybody really wants to move it anyway. The first thing we're going to do now is take photographs. Look ahead at Figure 1-2 for just a minute. Imagine yourself standing just inside the front—south—door. Check your camera for the number of the next exposure. Now take a picture pointing the camera just to the left, getting a little view of the kitchen. Stop *immediately* and make a note telling what this exposure showed, as well as what kind of film and what f-stop you used. If you work with different cameras at different times, you might even note what camera you were using. Your note might look like this:

> Roll 1. Exposure 8. 816 North Jackson. Int. kitchen taken from front door. Minolta 35mm SRT-100 w/50mm lens. Kodak Tri-X Pan ASA 400 27 DIN. f-16 @ 1/60 sec. with strobe.

I was still using black-and-white film in those days. Now, of course, crime scenes are photographed in color except in the very smallest and poorest departments. But — in real life — a police officer or private investigator will know what kind of film s/he is using. There's more about cameras and film in chapter nine.

If you know enough about photography to know what most of the information I gave means, you'll also want to know that in general, you'll be going for the greatest depth of field possible. The few exceptions occur when you are taking close-up photos of small items, wounds, weapons, fingerprints, footprints, and so forth. Then you'll probably be wanting to home in on the important feature and blur out just about everything else.

If things like ASA and DIN and f-stops don't mean anything to you, either read a good camera book or forget about them. You don't necessarily need them to write mysteries.

A lot more information than anybody reasonably should want? Sure it is — but who ever said defense attorneys were reasonable? If you don't have all that information, sooner or later some attorney is going to say, reproachfully, "Now, Officer So-and-So, tell the truth. Did you actually take these photographs?"

Of course you don't have to repeat all the information in every note, if you're taking photos in a sequence. Here's how your next couple of notes might look:

> Exposure 9. 816 North Jackson. Int. kitchen, part of table, taken from front door.
> Exposure 10. 816 North Jackson. Part of table, part of west wall, part of bathroom door, taken from front door.

This is assuming the rest of the information has not changed. When it does, your note will look like this:

> Roll 2. Exposure 4. 816 North Jackson. Exterior, north wall taken from back property line. f-22 1/200 sec. without strobe.

The assumption here is that you are still using the same camera and lens and, although you have changed rolls, you are still using the same *type* of film.

When you write your report, all this information will be included. Nit-picking? Sure it is. But in real life, there is too much at stake to take chances. In fiction, play it however you want to, for whatever your reasons are. Certainly very little of this information will actually turn up in any given story or novel—but it's useful to know what you can do with it if the information is recorded incorrectly.

Pan—that means rotate—the camera a little to the right, but stop when you still overlap the first shot. Take a second photograph and make all your notes again. When you've shot all the way around the room—which might take eight to twelve *overlapping* photographs—walk *directly* across the room, so that you're facing your original position, and take a picture of it. In a larger house you will need to do this in *each* room that could be related to the crime.

Now you'll take the camera outside (see Figure 1-3). Take one photograph each from the north, the south, the east, and the west of the house itself, and one each from the north, the south, the east, and the west of the bamboo thicket—or whatever you have in your crime scene.

As in this case it appears likely that the victim was carried out the back door into the bamboo thicket, take pictures of the back door from inside and from outside. Then, from the back door, take a picture of the bamboo thicket. Walk toward the bamboo thicket, taking pictures at about two-foot intervals. When you have reached the body, take at least one photograph each from left, from right, from top, from bottom, and from above, looking directly down.

In this case there is nothing unusual about the body you need to photograph now. If there were bullet or stab wounds, or defense wounds (we'll get to that later), you'd photograph them now.

Sketch and Measure

Next we have to take measurements and make sketches, both inside and outside. For the moment—look, we too like to breathe once in a while—we'll go inside, where the air is a little better.

We'll begin with a rough sketch (see Figure 1-1), getting in all the measurements so that we can make a finished drawing later for court if the case goes to court. To take the measurements, put you at one end of the tape measure and Mel (remember Mel, your part-

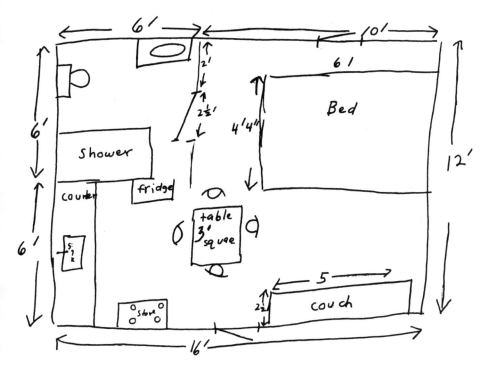

Figure 1-1. Rough crime-scene sketch. If there were anything of significance on the walls, they also would be shown, in "exploded out" format, as if a cardboard box were cut open and spread out.

ner?) at the other end of the tape measure. If you must do it by yourself, you can step it off—learn the length of your normal stride—but that is far from ideal.

As you can tell, it is very rough indeed; in fact, not all of it is fully legible. (That word that meant to be *stove* might just as well be *shave*.) But that's okay, because this drawing goes in your notebook, your case file. You'll make a better drawing later for the D.A. to see. You'll do that one sitting at your desk, using things like rulers, compasses, protractors—yep, those same things you learned how to use in the seventh grade, and weren't they fun?

In some larger police departments, they've even gone over to using computers to make crime-scene drawings. I never worked on a department that big, and chances are your fictional detective—if s/he's a cop at all—doesn't either. But if you're writing about New York or Los Angeles or Chicago, or their environs, you might want to call and be sure.

You may be thinking, now, that you don't need to make these drawings, because you're not working a real crime; you're writing a book.

Oh, yeah?

I've found that if I don't make a realistic drawing of every one of my fictional crime scenes, I wind up forgetting where things are, which direction doors open, and even where the body was. While I'm about it, I make maps of every location I made up, and get out maps of every real place I'm talking about. It's easy—and sloppy—to say it doesn't matter that much, it's only fiction. And it may be true that no more than one reader out of a thousand will catch you on the errors. But you'll know the difference. Martin Cruz Smith, who began as a mystery writer, says to writers' groups that integrity in writing is critical, and if you don't have it, you'll know it, and your work will show it.

Giving your fictional crime scene the care you'd give a real one is one way to maintain that integrity.

The final sketch (see Figure 1-2) is still not terrific, but that's okay. This is as good as it needs to be, most of the time. If you get Melvin Belli as a defense attorney you might want a much better drawing, but in that case you might have to ask a professional artist to do it. Most detectives—public sector or private—aren't extremely good at art.

In some cases, nothing outside is of immense importance. How-

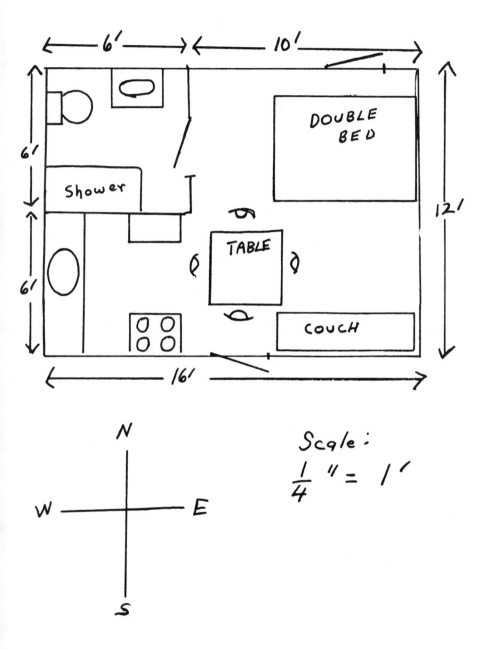

Figure 1-2. Finished crime-scene sketch. As in the rough sketch, if there were anything significant on the walls, they too would be shown.

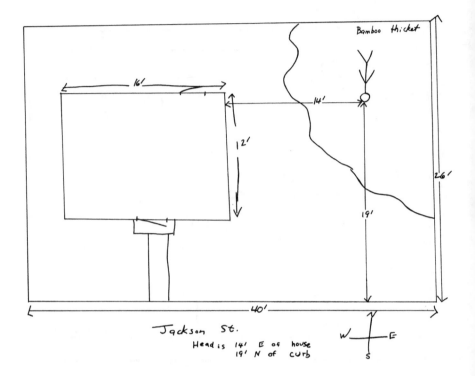

Figure 1-3. Outside crime-scene sketch.

ever, in this case, although the killing almost certainly took place indoors, the body was found outside. That means measurements and a sketch of the exterior also are necessary (see Figure 1-3).

Notice that the position of the body is *triangulated* — that is, measured from two fixed points, so that its location can be described absolutely accurately.

Now, you've got all the photographs and all the sketches and measurements you need to start with. Tell the EMT's they can move the body.

What do you mean they'd just as soon not? Do they expect it to stay here till next January? Hey, fellas, come and take it away.

Now.

It's gone. The place doesn't smell appreciably better.

TABLE 1
Who Does What When?

Dispatch—
- Receives initial telephoned complaint.
- Responds calmly to emergency situations.
- Provides help as possible over the phone.
- Sends patrol units and other essential personnel to scene.
- Receives reports from patrol units.
- Sends additional personnel to scene as need is reported.
- Coordinates car chases or foot chases, keeping units advised of each other's situation and location at all times.
- Maintains log of all calls.
- Retains tape recordings of all significant matters until they are disposed of.
- Knows whereabouts of all officers at all times.
- Prepares and dispatches updated lookout bulletins.
- On officers' requests, checks National Crime Information Center and other computerized data bases for wants and other information.
- As necessary, coordinates own department's efforts with efforts of other departments.
- Testifies in court as necessary.

Patrol Division—
- Gets the initial call.
- Goes to the scene and determines the situation.
- Gets initial information from complainant.
- Asks dispatch to send whoever else is needed.
- Contains witnesses.
- Controls scene.
- Makes arrest if perp is immediately visible.
- Chases perp if perp is attempting to escape.
- Assists detectives when they arrive.

- Makes initial report.
- Testifies in court as needed.

Detective Division —

- Goes to scene of major crimes.
- Asks dispatch to send whoever else is needed that patrol has not sent for.
- Interviews witnesses at scene.
- Instructs patrol division in more ways to help.
- Canvasses area to look for more possible witnesses.
- Arranges transport for witnesses to headquarters.
- Takes written statements from witnesses.
- Does follow-up investigation, which may take days, weeks, months or years.
- Prepares necessary search warrants and/or arrest warrants.
- Maintains case files.
- Writes follow-up reports as needed.
- Usually makes subsequent arrest.
- Coordinates with prosecuting attorney to be sure case is adequately presented.
- Testifies in court as needed.

Crime-Scene Division —

- Goes to scene of crimes and accidents.
- Takes photographs as appropriate.
- Develops photographs or arranges for them to be developed at secure facility.
- Makes measurements as appropriate.
- Makes initial crime-scene sketch at location.
- Makes detailed crime-scene drawing at headquarters.
- Collects physical evidence.
- Maintains legal integrity of physical evidence by
  1. Keeping evidence locker secure
  2. Maintaining chain of custody
  3. Keeping unauthorized people out.
- Prepares laboratory requests.

- Transports evidence to laboratory or arranges for its shipment certified mail, return receipt requested.
- Looks for fingerprints at scene and on evidence transported to headquarters.
- Maintains inked fingerprint and palm print files.
- Compares latent fingerprints to known prints of suspects.
- Searches unknown latent fingerprints through files, using all means available including computers.
- Prepares fingerprint charts.
- Testifies in court as needed.

Emergency Medical Technician —
- Examines victim at the scene, if there is any possibility the victim is alive.
- Provides emergency medical care.
- Transports victim to hospital, if victim is alive.
- Stays on hand to transport victim to morgue, if victim is dead.
- Testifies in court as necessary.

Coroner and/or Medical Examiner —
- Pronounces victim dead at scene.
- May make initial medical examination at scene.
- Arranges for and/or performs autopsy.
- Determines cause of death.
- Provides as much information as possible to investigating officers.
- Makes formal autopsy report.
- Testifies in court as necessary.

Coroner's or Medical Examiner's Investigator —
- Investigates cause of death, coordinating efforts with those of other investigators.
- Makes any necessary follow-up investigations as to exact cause of death.
- Testifies in court as necessary.

K-9 Unit —
- Dog may track apparent victim who has left scene.

- Dog may track perp who has left scene.
- Dog and trainer may help to control the scene.
- Dog may help to capture perp who is resisting arrest.
- Dog may sniff out drugs.
- Dog may sniff out explosives.
- Trainer testifies in court as necessary.

Secretary—

- Types and files reports dictated by officers.
- Types search warrants and arrest warrants, under direction of officers.
- Types and files written statements of witnesses, victims and perps, under direction of officers.
- Helps keep witnesses calm while statements are being taken.
- Deals with telephone and face-to-face inquiries from reporters, relatives and other interested persons.
- Testifies in court as necessary.

Crime-Laboratory Technician—

- May go to scene if crime is unusually serious.
- Receives evidence from crime-scene technician, maintaining proper chain of custody.
- Keeps evidence legally secure.
- Performs necessary chemical, radiological and/or microscopic examination of physical evidence.
- Makes detailed report to jurisdiction(s) involved with case.
- Testifies in court as necessary.

Records Division—

- Maintains mug shots and arrest records of all people arrested.
- Maintains copies of all initial and subsequent crime and accident reports, making them available to appropriate people including victims and their families, insurance companies, and officers from other jurisdictions.
- Makes out intake sheet on all arrestees.
- Fingerprints and photographs all arrestees.
- Microfilms old files so that the paper files can be placed in

long-range storage or discarded.
- Testifies in court as necessary.
- Keeps track of disposition of cases, so that records remain up to date.

District Attorney—
- Coordinates with investigating officers to be certain warrants are not taken before the case is adequately investigated.
- May provide additional investigators to work with police investigators to ensure that all legalities are dealt with appropriately.
- Prepares and presents case in court.

Be aware that not all jurisdictions have all of these positions, and that some of the names may differ from place to place. A person who investigates a crime may be called a detective or an investigator; that person may carry the rank of patrol officer first class or lieutenant, and the office that person works in may be called the Detective Division, the Detective Bureau or the Investigative Section. A person who goes to the crime scene for the purpose of taking photographs and measurements, sketching and fingerprinting may be called an identification officer, an identification technician or a scene-of-crimes officer.

As a writer, you have the responsibility of checking with the appropriate police department, district attorney's office, sheriff's department, or whatever to determine precisely what is done in the kind of department you are writing about.

Failing to look into these matters can result in your looking extremely stupid—in print.

T W O

CRIME-SCENE SEARCH

There is little probability of finding anything of importance if the attention be confined to safes, beds, boxes, stoves, or chimneys. Absolutely everything must be examined, for there is no place where important objects cannot be hidden. The following for example are a few of the hiding places discovered by the author or his friends: — the horsehair stuffing of a sofa, a birdcage, the space between the back of a picture and its protecting board, the hole of an old key, the manger in a stable, a pot in which soup was actually boiling on the fire (it contained 28 gold coins), a prayer-book, old boots, a dog kennel, the space between two upright millstones, wine barrels, a spectacle case, a pill-box, old newspapers, a cuckoo clock, a baby's clothes; and on one occasion the criminal himself was discovered in a dung heap, a small opening having been made to give him air in the side nearest to the stable wall.

— Hans Gross,
Criminal Investigation

Dr. Hans Gross, professor of criminology at the University of Prague, has the distinction of having written the very first book of criminology that was a major influence in the Western world. Originally titled *Handbuch fur Untersuchungsrichter als System der Kriminalistik (A Handbook on the Criminal Sciences for Examining Magistrates)* and published in the last quarter of the nineteenth century, it went through countless translations and new editions; the 1934 English translation of the third edition, which I quote here, was a very late version. Although almost everything in it is now outdated and superseded, it is still well worth reading because it was the first solid attempt to systemize investigation and turn it into a science.

The situation Gross describes in the preceding passage has not changed in the slightest. Some of the unlikely places my friends and I have found evidence include a hole in the outside wall of a house on the escape route of a robber, a residential garbage can in the alley two blocks from where the crime occurred, the inside top of a lipstick tube (an Avon special, made for holding solid cologne as well as a lipstick), inside sugar and flour canisters, inside refrigerators and freezers, inside an ornamental clock, and inside curtain rods. Narcotics officers once searched a house for marijuana and hashish without success, but totally missed the six marijuana plants growing in small pots on the kitchen counter. (Dell Shannon—in real life, Elizabeth Linington—put that one in a book, after I told her about it.)

Secret documents, jewels and drugs have been smuggled inside baby's diapers, inside corpses being returned home for burial, in balloons swallowed or thrust up the courier's anus, inside linings or hems of clothing, in cameras and film containers, inside ballpoint pens or fountain pens. Disassembled weapons have been smuggled disguised as camera components; assembled and disassembled weapons have been shipped in bags of flour, meal or powdered milk, in barrels of missionary clothing, in crates of tools and hardware. In fiction, hide contraband anywhere you like. You can be sure some real criminal has thought of it before you.

Collecting evidence deserves a special chapter—or more—of its own. In real life, it is critical that evidence be collected and treated correctly, if it is to tell what it can tell. In fiction, you have to know what you can and can't do with evidence—but bear in mind that this is something that changes. Keep track of court decisions and technical developments to keep your writing current.

A person searching a crime scene is less likely than someone searching a suspect's house to find evidence deliberately hidden, unless the scene also involved narcotics, smuggling, the concealment of stolen property, or something like that. Also, a person searching a crime scene doesn't need a search warrant if someone who has control over the area is willing to sign a consent-to-search form.

If no one is willing, or legally able, to sign a consent-to-search form, then a search warrant is essential.

Searching With a Warrant

For clarity, let's assume again that you are your fictional investigator. Here is how you get and use a search warrant:

1. You must be a law-enforcement officer. No search warrant can be issued to anyone who is not a law-enforcement officer.

2. You must prepare an affidavit, in duplicate, describing the area

to be searched, the items you intend to search for, and why you expect to find those items in that location (*probable cause*). Prepare a search warrant, in triplicate. Take the affidavits and warrants to a judge and swear to the affidavits. At that time, if the judge thinks your cause is probable enough, the judge signs the search warrants. The judge keeps one copy of the affidavit; you keep the other, along with all three copies of the search warrant.

3. You and however many more people you need go to the scene. Unless the scene is already under the control of the police, as it usually is when you're searching the scene of a crime, or unless you have a no-knock warrant—which is issued only if there is strong reason to suspect evidence will be destroyed in the time it takes for someone to open the door, or strong reason to fear for the safety of the officers serving the warrant—you knock on the door, announce yourselves as police officers, and wait for somebody to come to the door.

4. Usually one officer (or more, if necessary) will corral all people on the scene and keep them confined to one area. It is courteous and good public relations, though not a legal requirement, to avoid frightening children or other innocent people unnecessarily.

5. Search for the items on the list. Make a list on the warrant itself—in triplicate, because that's how many copies of the warrants you have—of everything seized whether or not it was on the original list of items sought for.

6. You are not responsible for restoring the premises to their presearch condition. However, you should avoid unnecessary damage and take all reasonable precautions for safeguarding property that belongs on the scene.

7. Leave one copy of the warrant, complete with detailed list of items seized, with the people in control of the place you searched. If nobody is there, leave a copy of the warrant displayed in a prominent place. Keep one warrant for your files, and return one to the court that issued the warrant.

Be aware that when officers are searching with a warrant (and remember that your private eye or your brilliant amateur cannot get a search warrant), the warrant must describe the places they may look and the items they may look for. Among other things, this means that unless the warrant mentions "the house and all outbuildings" instead of just "the house" nobody may search the garage or the lawn mower shed. Unless the warrant also mentions vehicles, officers may search the garage but not the car parked in the garage. If the smallest item mentioned on the search warrant is a refrigerator, no one may search the junk drawer in the kitchen — and if someone does search the junk drawer in the kitchen and find a pistol, that's tough. It is tainted evidence, not admissible in court, even if it is the weapon that was used to kill that officer's closest friend. However, an officer looking for a pistol who finds a stolen refrigerator may use that evidence, because there is no place the refrigerator would have fit that it would not have been reasonable to look for the pistol.

Furthermore — and this comes directly from the Constitution's Fourth Amendment, part of the Bill of Rights — the search warrant may be issued only on the basis of probable cause, listing what officers expect to find there and why they expect to find those items, and suspicion isn't probable cause. If an officer saw fifteen known drug wholesalers and twenty known dealers and thirty other people carrying cash and packages entering and leaving a suspect location in twenty minutes, chances are a judge will issue a search warrant. But if all the officer has is the fact that the owner of the house looks scruffy and there has been a lot of coming and going there in the middle of the night, almost certainly a search warrant will not be granted.

In the case of a crime scene, a crime is known to have occurred in that location and officers are looking for all evidence having to do with the crime. Generally, this is sufficient probable cause unless a judge rules otherwise. Judges are highly unpredictable.

The most common basis for issuing a search warrant in a situation not involving an obvious crime scene is the word of an informant. Although courts have ruled that the warrant, and the affidavit given in applying for the warrant, do not have to list the informant's name, the paperwork should specify that this is an informant whose information has in the past proven accurate. (This means that the first time or two that a particular informant is used, there must be some other source of the same information.)

An officer working with an informant should try to get the informant to list as small an item as possible because, remember, the smaller the smallest item listed is, the greater the scope of places the officer may look.

Exceptions to the Rule

There are exceptions to the rule requiring search warrants. If there is strong probable cause and the place to be searched is highly portable—a car, a boat, an airplane—in some situations the officer may reasonably search without a warrant. But if the situation is such that the vehicle can be impounded while a warrant is issued, then the search may not proceed without the warrant. I wrote a novel, *The Eye of Anna,* in which an officer searched a house without a warrant because he had strong probable cause to believe that a murderer had been holed up in the house, a hurricane was in progress, and the officer had reason to believe the house might be blown away before he could finish the search. (It was.) In real life, could he have gotten away with that? Danged if I know, but it was fun to write.

The other main exception is that if an officer has grounds to fear for his/her own personal safety, s/he may immediately search any area within the immediate physical control of the suspect for weapons. Often, officers stopping a car and searching the glove box under this exception find drugs instead of a weapon. Almost invariably, an immediate court battle ensues, arguing whether the officer had actual and reasonable cause to search for a weapon or whether the search for the weapon was merely an excuse to search for drugs. Courts have ruled differently in different situations, so this is a wide-open area to consider in writing fiction.

In real life, it is essential that no officer conduct a search alone. There should always be at least two people to testify as to what was found and who found it. Furthermore, the two people must always search together; it won't do any good, later in court, for Mel to testify that s/he was there when N.E. Boddy found the murder weapon, if Mel was outside or in another room and Boddy is accused of planting the weapon.

But this isn't a law book. Let's get on to what your character might find, how s/he should treat it and not treat it at the scene, and what can be done with it later in the lab. Always, always, always, remember that this information changes fast, so check with your real jurisdiction, or the closest real one to a fictitious one, at the time you are writing as to what can be done there at that time.

Identification and crime-scene officers are genial souls, almost always happy to tell you what they're doing and show you around, provided they don't have a call at the moment. (But do be aware that even if you have an appointment, you can't count on the officer being there. Crime takes precedence.)

Evidence Collection

For now, let's get on with evidence collection. How do officers collect different items of evidence? What do they do with them after collecting them? In this chapter, we'll discuss collecting and packaging the evidence. In chapter nine, we'll examine what the lab does with the evidence.

Expect the Unexpected

The only way an evidence technician can be prepared for anything is to be prepared for everything. Murder happens fast.

At the very least, an evidence collection kit must contain large, medium and small paper and plastic bags. If they are not preprinted with evidence tags (we'll get to those later), evidence tags can be attached with string or tape. The kit must contain paper coin envelopes, small vials of the type used by pharmacies to dispense tablets, and larger plastic or glass containers with airtight lids. Anything meant to contain liquids should be made of an inert material, so that the eyedropper and/or container will not leave its own chemical trace in the liquid, unless of course the lab already knows about and plans for the chemical trace, as in the case of some prepackaged kits. There should be a supply of cardboard boxes that can be set up to hold larger items; prepackaged kits for gunpowder residue, blood samples and rape analysis; vials with disposable eyedroppers fixed in the lids; dental casting material and equipment (the same stuff the dentist used to get the exact shape your bridge needed to be), and plaster casting material and equipment. Tweezers and scissors are essential. Obviously, the kit must contain evidence tags and the long, yellow preprinted evidence tape to keep people out of the immediate crime scene (although it's usually necessary, if it's a major crime, to post a few patrol officers on the perimeter also).

Rubber gloves are critical; I once caught pneumococcal pneumonia from a corpse, and in this day of AIDS, anybody who handles bloody items without wearing gloves is clearly suicidal.

Of course you already know your character will need notebook, pens, pencils, tape measures, a camera and strobe, and plenty of film and batteries.

It is useful to have several heavy-duty cardboard boxes with pegboard bases, and a number of long, heavy nails to put through the bottom of the pegboard, so that oddly-shaped items may be securely immobilized.

This kit should be kept at all times in the vehicle that will be used. Each time the kit is used it must be *immediately* restocked, to be ready for its next use. Obviously, if the vehicle must go into the shop, the kit must be moved to the substitute vehicle. Murder happens fast and it doesn't give the unprepared person time to say "Oops, let me get my stuff together." An officer who isn't prepared to go with no advance warning whatever and spend the next ten hours working a major crime scene, photographing, measuring, charting and collecting upwards of 500 pieces of numbered and labeled evidence, without sending a patrol officer out to an all-night drugstore to get something s/he forgot, isn't prepared at all.

That doesn't mean your fictional character really has to be that well prepared. Sometimes a lack of preparation may add to the drama of the story—but remember that it also must be consistent with your character or story line. Either the character is perennially forgetful or lazy (like Joyce Porter's Dover), or the character has just finished with one major crime and is too dog-tired to remember to restock instantly.

Each Item Packaged Separately

When collecting evidence, the technician must package each item separately. This includes, for example, putting each shoe in a separate labeled evidence bag if a pair of shoes is being collected. If a victim's clothing is being collected, each item of clothing goes in a separate bag. (Yes, that includes each sock. It is appropriate to handle them with tweezers.) It is critical to label each item the moment it is collected, and to make corresponding notes in the technician's notebook immediately. Trusting it to memory and planning to write it up later is extremely stupid; memory cannot be trusted that far, especially by someone who has other things on his/her mind.

Paper or Plastic?

How does your character decide whether to use paper or plastic to collect the evidence?

If the item is likely to be even slightly damp, it must be packaged in paper so that the moisture can continue to evaporate; otherwise, the item is likely to begin to rot. Clothing with blood on it is a special problem. It should not be folded in on itself; rather, it must be spread out and allowed to dry. In Albany, Georgia, where I worked for nearly seven years, this was a big problem for a long time; there were times when we had no usable interrogation rooms because they all were full of bloody clothing drying out. (And one rather hysterical day, one detective ushered a suspect into an interrogation room another detective had just put a suspect shotgun in. Fortunately, the suspect was a rather mild-mannered burglar, and on seeing the shotgun he backed out in a hurry.)

But we had one unexpected and somewhat serendipitous stroke of luck. One day a city commissioner walked through the city parking garage and saw Doc Luther, head of the crime-scene unit, and me fingerprinting a suspect vehicle. He stopped short. "Don't you have a better place to do that?" he demanded.

"No, sir, we do not," Doc told him. "Not unless we want to do it outside." (The day was rainy. Fingerprint powder and rain do not combine well.)

The commissioner asked more questions, and Doc let him have the situation: We had already lost one case in court because we were fingerprinting a car full of stolen property when the suspect walked by. Although in fact the suspect did not touch any of the stolen property at that time, he managed to convince a jury that he did and that was how his fingerprints got there. Even Doc and I had to admit that the suspect had been close enough that he *could* have touched the property. He mentioned the problem with bloody clothing—which should have been our responsibility, but we had no place to deal with it—drying in interrogation rooms. He explained that the problems were getting worse, as crime in the city expanded at a geometric rate.

"I'll take care of that," the commissioner said.

A few months later, we had a nice building at the bottom of the parking lot. It was big enough for us to fingerprint even a large suspect vehicle and to process and store other large evidence. From then on, bloody clothing was dried and stored there.

If your officer is working in a small jurisdiction, by all means use the problems of small departments. Things can't be done exactly right, and there are tremendous fictional opportunities there.

Nothing with blood on it should ever be packaged in plastic or glass or anything else airtight, unless it is the blood itself and it is put in special vials that already contain a known blood preservative. The laboratories can work easily with dried blood or with properly preserved blood, but not with rotted blood.

Dry items may be packaged in plastic, although no particular harm is done if they are packaged in paper. Something that may need to be repeatedly examined, such as a pistol, should always be in transparent plastic, so that it can be examined without the police seal being broken. Obviously, any time the seal is broken—for fingerprinting or test-firing—notations should be made on the evidence tag, so that the defense attorney can't question later why there are two or three sets of staple holes.

Learning to pick things up without damaging fingerprints that might be on them is an art. It generally involves using only the fingertips to pick up items and holding them by edges that are too small to hold prints (see Figure 2-1); there is really no way to learn without practicing. Try it yourself, so as to know the problems your character is facing.

Let's go on, now, talking for a few paragraphs as if you are your character.

Once you have succeeded in picking up the item, the next problem is packaging it without rubbing out the fingerprints. If the item is absorbent, there is no problem at all. Those prints aren't going anywhere. They are in the substance, not just on the surface, of the item. However, you must be extremely careful not to touch the items yourself, as even the most casual touch will add more prints. These things are best handled with tweezers at all times.

If the item is irregularly shaped, there's really little problem, because the protrusions will hold the paper or plastic away from the rest of the surface and keep it from rubbing out prints. But when you have something regularly shaped—a drinking glass, a pane of glass—you may have problems, because plastic will tend to mold around the item and rub out prints. Paper works better, especially ordinary brown paper grocery-type sacks, because they are too stiff to rub out prints unless the item is badly mishandled. In actual practice, Doc and I tended to print small items on the scene whenever possible, and then transport them (if necessary—often the prints were all we needed, and the item could be left at the scene) with fingerprints already protected by tape. With larger, heavier

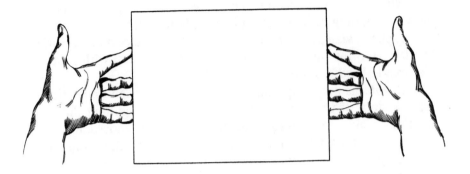

Figure 2-1. Holding pane of glass by outside edges only, using fingertips only. Illustration by Tom Post.

items, there is no problem, because these items will be transported in boxes and there is no chance of the boxes' rubbing out prints.

Of course, with extremely large items, there may also be a problem, because it may be impossible to move the item without touching areas that might hold prints. In that case, it is essential to print the areas that must be touched, then move the item, and then finish the work in the lab. What if the item is outside and it's raining? Then you go crazy for a while. Honestly—I can't provide advice. You just assess the situation and try to do whatever will be least harmful to the evidence, then hope you haven't missed something vital.

For dramatic purposes, you may decide instead to have your character do whatever is *most* harmful to the evidence, either by accident, deliberately, or because the situation is so bad it cannot be redeemed.

Often, detectives brought us pieces of broken glass, holding them carefully by the edges, to have the surfaces printed. In a case like that, generally the detective would lay the glass on the seat beside him in the car on the way in, and hand it to us with a separate evidence tag for us to attach later. This worked well; the car's seat covers were too stiff to damage any prints, and it would take us only minutes to print the item and attach the tag.

This Glass is Full of—Something

Now suppose you need to fingerprint a container that is full of an unknown liquid. You will eventually have to get an analysis of the liquid, so you can't just dump it. You can't fingerprint the container with the liquid in it, because examining an item while fingerprinting it involves turning it in different directions to get the light on it at different angles.

Being able to pick up a glass, cup or bottle by the rim and the angle where the side and the base join—using only your fingertips—and pour the contents into another container takes a lot of practice (see Figure 2-2). But that is the only way to do it. After that, the glass or cup must completely air dry before fingerprinting begins. (No, you should not use a hair dryer on it. The resultant heat and rapid moisture evaporation could harm any remaining fingerprints.) This in turn means that very often it must be transported into the police station with the dregs of the liquid still in it—which means that it must be packaged and transported right side up.

For collecting some evidence, there are special kits you can

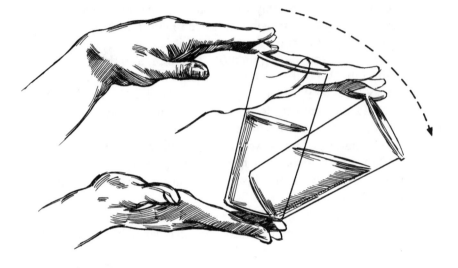

Figure 2-2. Holding glass with fingertips only to pour liquid out. Left fingertips just touch top edge of glass; right fingertips just touch bottom edge. Practice this with an unbreakable glass in a spill-proof location. Illustration by Tom Post.

buy from suppliers or, sometimes, obtain from the crime lab. To collect blood samples in the preservative jar, simply unscrew the lid, collect the sample with the enclosed eyedropper, and screw the lid down again. The directions that come with the kit tell you which items do and do not need to be refrigerated. (After we got a refrigerator in the lab, many a day Doc, Butch and I stored our lunches in the same refrigerator that might be containing biological samples waiting to be transported to the lab. We were, of course, careful that everything—including lunches and samples—was properly packaged.)

A rape kit has to be kept refrigerated after use, and it should be transported to the lab as soon as possible. The officer or evidence technician does not personally use the rape kit; rather, s/he takes it to the hospital and turns it over to the examining physician, who will use the kit. (Preferably, the examination will be performed in the presence of a female officer, to cut down on the chain of evidence, unless the officer's presence is too distressing to the victim.) Following the examination, the physician turns the kit back over to the officer. The rape kit contains fine-toothed combs, tapes and vials to collect swabs from several pubic areas, vaginal washings and combings, and loose hairs that might be those of the suspect. These critical bits of evidence are the reason police ask the victim not to bathe until after she has been medically examined; very often the victim will then shower right in the hospital before putting on the fresh clothes she has taken with her. All the clothing she was wearing at the time of the assault and immediately after it will be turned over to the police in hopes that some hair, fiber and/or semen from the assailant remains on it.

Shoe Prints, Tire Tracks

Shoe prints and tire tracks are first photographed with a special camera on a frame that points directly down. Because the camera is on a frame, the ratio of the negative to the original (that is, the relationship in terms of size) is known, and the original track can be exactly reproduced in size. After that, the officer should make casts, often called moulages, of them. S/he begins by spraying the surface with a fixative; ordinary hair spray or shellac will do in a pinch, but a special fixative available from supply houses is preferable. Then a portable frame—metal or wood—is placed around the track. Using the bucket and stirring stick that is part of his/her equipment, and following package directions on the bag of plaster, the officer mixes the plaster with water obtained at the scene. (Someone who habitually goes places where water is not readily available should carry several gallons of water in the trunk of his/her car.) Very carefully, pouring onto the stirring stick held just above the print in order to break the flow and diffuse the plaster mixture and keep it from damaging the print, the officer pours the plaster into the frame. The plaster is reinforced with twigs, straw, and so forth from the scene; an officer who customarily goes places where s/he cannot expect to find twigs and straw should carry Popsicle sticks, available in bulk in craft stores under the name of "craft sticks," as a substitute. It is important to avoid using twigs and straw from a different location, as that might confuse scientists who are studying the shoes and tires and the casts.

Waiting for the plaster to dry may take anywhere from ten minutes to two hours, depending on the quality of the plaster and the atmospheric conditions. When it is nearly dry, a twig or even a finger is used as a stylus to put the officer's initials, the date and the case number in the back of the plaster. When it is completely dry, the casting is carefully lifted and put into a cardboard box upside down to finish drying. The officer should not try to clean it; that is left for the lab to do. This procedure accomplishes two things at once: it provides a cast of the shoe or tire, and it provides an exact sample of the soil, with its associated leaves, twigs and debris, in which the print was made, for comparison to the soil adhering to the shoe or tire.

Toolmarks

An officer should never attempt to fit a suspect tool into a toolmark; doing so would damage the evidence. If at all possible, the item the toolmark is on should be collected and packaged for transmittal to the lab. The crime-scene kit should contain a small saw, so that officers can, if necessary, saw out a section of the door frame where the pry mark is located. (I once moved into an apartment and noticed immediately that a section of an interior door frame had been sawed out and neatly painted over and several circles of carpet had been taken out and replaced with carpet almost, but not quite, matching in color. That alerted me that a major crime of some sort had occurred in that apartment.)

If removal of the area is absolutely impossible, dental casting material can be used to obtain an exact cast of the print. The officer must follow directions on the container, as there are many different types of dental casting material.

Fibers, Soil, Hair, Leaves, Pollen, Fireclay

Any piece of small evidence that is big enough to see, no matter what it is, should be collected with tweezers and put into coin envelopes (if there is the slightest possibility that it is even slightly damp) or into small plastic bags.

But what about the ones that are too small to see?

This is when an *evidence vacuum*, a small, extremely powerful vacuum cleaner equipped with filters, is useful. The vacuum cleaner is first cleaned, even if it is always cleaned after use, just in case somebody else forgot to do it last time. Then the officer inserts the first filter, and choosing a small, easily definable section, such as the floorboard, passenger's side, front seat, s/he vacuums up *everything* in that area. Then that filter with its entire contents is placed in an evidence bag, the vacuum cleaner is cleaned again, the second filter is inserted, and the work continues.

If the same area is going to be fingerprinted, it is essential to use the evidence vacuum before fingerprinting, to avoid contaminating the vacuum sweepings with fingerprint powder. Obviously, it takes something of a contortionist to vacuum an area without touching it, but ident people learn to do such things.

Soil and Leaf Samples Outdoors

Samples are collected from every area the perp would have contacted. Each one is packaged separately; both the evidence tag and the officer's notes should tell *exactly* where each sample came from. Triangulation is crucial in case someone else should have to locate the exact same spot again.

Broken Glass

You already know how glass is collected without damaging fingerprints. Your officer will be sure to identify, in notes and on the evidence tag, exactly where each fragment came from. The lab needs that information.

Blood Spatters

Blood spatters can be few and widely scattered; they can be widely dispersed over a large area. Totally accurate photography and measurements are critical. In a case in Cincinnati, a man was stabbed in the lung. Blood in the lung mixed with the air and sprayed through the exit wound, so that a fine, almost imperceptible mist of blood covered the immediate area. Detectives observed that an area of floor was *not* sprayed; from that they were able to ascertain the shape of the perp's jacket, and to deduce that when they found the perp's jacket, it would have blood on it. In other cases—these involving stabbing or bashing—detectives have been able to determine from the pattern of blood spattering the height and even the hand preference of the perp, and—again—to know that certain items of clothing will have blood on them.

Not all blood is red; not all blood tracings are visible. Large amounts of blood, after being exposed to air for several hours, turn to a very glossy black and tend to dry in stacks and then crack, so that the floor will appear to be covered by irregular stacks of glossy black tile. In other situations, blood may turn pinkish, brownish or even greenish. It is very difficult to scrub all the blood up; even after the walls and floors appear immaculate to the naked eye, spraying the area with a chemical called luminol (which is available in several different trademarked packagings) will cause all areas where blood has been to fluoresce. In such a case, taking up the floorboards, tile or carpet will usually disclose puddles of blood lying on the subflooring. It may also be necessary to take apart the plumbing and look for blood traces in the sink traps.

Smaller spatters of blood should be allowed to dry naturally, even if that involves keeping the scene sealed and guarded for several days. Then each one should be measured, rephotographed, traced in complete detail and carefully triangulated not only in location, but also in exact position within that location (is the spray coming from up or down, left or right?). Then, if possible, the surface containing the spatters should be removed to the lab.

What can the lab do with the spatters? We'll get to all that later, in chapter nine, which tells what the lab does, and in the appendices, which provide sample lab reports.

Let's go on, now, to firearms. They deserve a section all their own.

TABLE 2
Processing the Crime Scene

These pages come from the Evidence Collection Manual, *published by Sirchie Finger Print Laboratories, Inc., and are used by permission. The charts have been edited for use in this publication.*

The following is a brief procedural guideline for collecting and preserving physical evidence at the scene of a crime. Any number of commercially available journals provide excellent detailed information regarding the science of evidence collection. We strongly recommend our Sirchie TB300, *Evidence Collection Mission*, as an outstanding source of detailed information.

Clear the area: Clear all except essential and authorized persons from the crime-scene area. This includes all officers who are not needed for specific functions. The more people present, the more chance for damage or loss of evidence.

Use a systematic approach: Use caution when searching for evidence. Study the whole crime-scene area first, since the relationship of different exhibit positions may be important. Systematically cover the crime scene so that nonobvious or hidden evidence is not overlooked. Speed and carelessness may lead to overlooking evidence or to the damage or destruction of important exhibits.

Limit the number of evidence collectors: Designate one, or at most a pair, of officers to collect all evidence. This places responsibility on specific individuals. It will also tend to avoid confusion at some later date as to who recovered specific items and where they were found.*

Photograph the evidence: Take photographs as necessary prior to moving or securing exhibits.

Use common sense: Use knowledge, experience and intelligence in collecting evidence. Consider what significance the exhibit may have and what examinations the laboratory may conduct. With this in mind, the trained investigator will normally be able to correctly secure and preserve the exhibits.

Keep accurate records: Prepare notes or other records as items

*Author's note: This does *not* mean that only one person should *search.* Rather, it means that in the search team, one person should be responsible for *collecting* the finds.

are collected. Record the item, its condition (if appropriate), the exact location relative to a fixed and permanent position, the date, the time, etc.

Mark the exhibits: Place permanent and distinctive marks directly on the objects collected if this is possible without damaging the evidence.

Mark the containers: When unable to mark the exhibit itself, such as in the case of stains, hair, paint, etc., place the evidence in a vial or small plastic or paper envelope, then seal and mark the container. Even when the exhibit itself can be marked, it is usually advisable to seal it in some kind of container and place additional identification marks on the container.

Keep the markings brief: Initials or the name of the officer collecting the evidence is essential. In marking containers, other pertinent data can be included, such as date, location where found, case number and description of the exhibit. Do not include extraneous information or conclusions of the investigator since these might render the label inadmissible as evidence in court.

Use proper containers:

1. Plastic or cellophane envelopes are excellent for small objects that are not organic in nature.

2. Paper envelopes are used for organic evidence (body fluids, biological evidence, etc.). *Note*: Air dry all evidence items before packaging.

Seal all corners adequately if very small or powdery material is enclosed. It is preferable to place the latter in plastic envelopes. Do not use paper envelopes for fiber evidence as the paper itself may contain fibers and thus contaminate the evidence.

3. Vials, pill boxes, capsules and like containers are frequently suitable, depending upon the exhibit and its condition.

4. Garments and large exhibits can be placed in bags or rolled in paper.

FIREARMS

The examination of firearms may require the assistance of a whole series of . . . experts.

— Hans Gross,
Criminal Investigation

You have undoubtedly seen investigators on television collecting a firearm by sticking a pencil or pen down the barrel. This is, to put it very mildly, not SOP—Standard Operating Procedure. (Remember the term. It's as important in police work as it is in the military.) In the first place, this procedure is unsafe; but even more important to criminal investigation, it could damage the inside of the barrel. The lands and grooves inside the barrel are the main—generally the only—way of definitely identifying which firearm fired which slug.

What Is a Firearm?

Let's back up a little. What do we mean when we say firearms? The more common term, of course, is *gun*. (Do not use *gun* to mean *rifle* in the Marine Corps. If you do, you will be required to spend several days walking around reciting to everyone you see an extremely vulgar little rhyme.)

Categories of Firearms

Firearms fall into two major categories, *small arms*, which include all the weapons normally used by civilians or police officers, and *artillery*, which means larger caliber weapons such as cannon and antiaircraft guns. Crimes almost never involve artillery, although a .50-caliber handgun recently invented in Utah may begin to blur the distinction. But for the time being we'll be thinking here of small arms, which include handguns and weapons normally fired from the shoulder.

Handguns

Revolver (although not technically a pistol, a revolver is often referred to colloquially as a pistol)
Semiautomatic pistol (usually referred to as automatic pistol)

Shoulder weapons

Breechblock Rifle
Bolt-Action Rifle
Lever-Action Rifle
Slide-Action Rifle
Semiautomatic Rifle
Automatic Rifle
Shotgun

A few combination weapons exist, the most common being a shotgun-rifle combination called an *over-and-under*, in which a rifle barrel and firing mechanism sits atop a shotgun barrel and firing mechanism. A double-barreled shotgun may be an over-and-under or a *side-by-side*, in which the two barrels are, as the name suggests, side by side.

The smallest readily available handgun, designed for concealment, is the Derringer. This weapon has a very short range and little accuracy. It would be useful only in resisting or making a sneak attack. Think of it as a "lady's weapon" (as opposed to a woman's weapon, which may be anything) or a "gambler's weapon."

Derringers in the classic style have one or two barrels, each with its own chamber and firing mechanism; another variety, the "pepperbox," has four. Derringer-like innovations include one-shot pistols disguised as fountain pens or miniflashlights; a similar item is a one-shot belt buckle fired by abdominal pressure. What it gains in sneakiness it loses in unwieldness.

Along the same lines are guns, knives, and stilettos disguised as belt buckles, compact cases, letter openers, keys, and just about anything else you want to name. Swords and single-shot rifles are built into umbrellas, canes and briefcases. Watching a few James Bond movies should give you more ideas.

There are some even less common weapons, generally no longer in production, such as the "lemon-squeezer" pistol (so called because it was cocked by squeezing the grips), that I don't intend to cover here. If you're thinking of writing about anything that esoteric, chances are you're into firearms anyway.

Ammunition

All these weapons fire *ammunition*. But at this point, the terminology begins to get a little confused. For the time being, forget about shotguns. We'll get to them later. Right now we're talking about all other small arms. In the military services, normally a single round of ammunition—that is, a single item to be loaded into a firearm—is called a *cartridge* and the portion propelled through the air is called a *bullet*; but in police terminology, normally what the military calls a *cartridge* is a *bullet* and what the military calls a *bullet* is a *slug*. Decide for yourself which terminology is more appropriate for what you're writing. I'll use them interchangeably in this book.

What is ammunition made of? Whether you want to call it a bullet or a cartridge, it has four main components:

- The casing or shell;

- The propellant (black powder, smokeless powder, nitrocellulose, or whatever);

- The primer (which is hit by the firing pin, ignites with an extremely hot flame, and ignites the propellant);

- The bullet or slug, which may be solid lead or lead jacketed with a thin layer of copper, steel or Teflon. The Teflon-coated bullets, which slip easily through bullet-proof vests and other body armor, are often referred to as *cop-killers*.

How does ammunition work? The rapid ignition (which actually is not quite an explosion) produces:

- A loud report (which can be muted to approximate a cough by a silencer on some but not all weapons);

- A simultaneous muzzle flash (which cannot be eliminated) and forward propulsion of the bullet;
- A mixture of hot gases and gunpowder residue that is propelled back toward the hand of the person holding the gun.

The heat

- Softens the bullet, forcing it to conform to the shape of the inside of the gun barrel.

How is a shotgun shell different? A shotgun shell is slightly different; instead of a slug, it contains:

- A primer;
- A load of gunpowder;
- Pellets called *shot*;
- *Wads*, pieces of cardboard or paper packed in the shell between the primer and the powder and between the powder and the shot.

In shotgun shells that are reloaded at home (check a large gun reference book for more about that), the wadding often is punched out of magazine pages. Many years ago in London, a police officer was murdered. At the scene, other officers found a partially burned fragment of the wadding, which came from an identifiable newspaper three years old. The search for the suspect continued for several years, but when a suspect was finally developed, officers located at his home both the pages the wadding was punched out of and additional shells loaded with wadding from those pages. This evidence proved to be the vital link to convicting the culprit. That sounds good to me. There's no reason you can't reuse it in fiction.

Rifling

With the exception of the shotgun, all these weapons have *rifled barrels*. Rifling, which was developed about five hundred years ago, consists of a series of wide spiral *grooves* cut into the gun-barrel. These grooves, by causing the basically cigar-shaped bullet to spiral through the air much the way a properly thrown football does, greatly improve the accuracy of flight; a smooth-bore firearm is extremely inaccurate at distances of over about eighty feet. (Now you know why you never could hit the side of a barn with a BB gun. It's smooth-bore.) The raised spaces between the grooves in the barrel are called *lands*. Because the heated slug conforms to and mirrors the shape of the inside of the barrel, the grooves will show up on the soft lead of the bullet (or slug) as shallow raised areas; the lands show up on the bullet as grooves cut into it. Although theoretically all the rifling on firearms manufactured in the same batch should be identical, actually, even to start with, there are microscopic differences, because the rifling equipment is worn slightly more with each barrel it rifles.

The more the firearm is fired, the more pronounced those differences become, as the inside of the barrel, reacting to the heat and the friction of the lead rushing through it, continues to wear. This means that it is possible to identify the slug that went through any given barrel. In practice, this means that it is usually possible to tell what slug was fired from any given gun. Although barrels in some firearms are interchangeable, rarely does anybody switch them—but a recent novel had a delightful scene in which a professional killer committed a murder and then he immediately disassembled his weapon, dropped the barrel and firing pin overboard into the Pacific Ocean, attached a new barrel and firing pin, and went on about his business.

In general, criminals don't do that. The pros might.

In real life: This is not to say there has never been a question as to whether a particular barrel was originally on a particular gun. In the still-controversial Sacco-Vanzetti case, there is no doubt that a barrel that is now on one of the revolvers in the case is the one through which the allegedly fatal bullet was fired, and that the revolvers were in the possession of Sacco and Vanzetti when they were arrested. What does remain in question, however, is whether those particular barrels were on those particular revolvers at the time, and whether the bullet that was presented in court was the one that killed either of the men or one that was later substituted. Proper chain of custody would have prevented those questions from arising.

The Examiner's Role

The arrangement of lands and grooves and the twist of the spiraling vary according to the caliber, make and model of a firearm. So, faced with an undamaged or lightly damaged slug fired from an unknown weapon, the firearms examiner can generally say, with a very high degree of certainty, what make, model and caliber of gun fired it. A severely damaged slug, of course, may make such identification impossible. The slug can be severely damaged in any one or more of several ways. First, it is hot as it leaves the gun barrel. As it flies through the air simultaneously piercing the air and spinning, it continues to be heated by the friction of the air molecules. A soft lead bullet, striking anything hard, will tend to *splat!* and distort quite a lot; a copper- or steel-jacketed bullet may distort less from the splat effect but may shatter if it hits bone or metal. On the other hand, even a soft lead bullet that passes through only soft tissue probably will have very little distortion.

A shotgun differs in this regard, in that, generally, the shot is not marked by the barrel. Therefore, it is not generally possible to say what load of shot came from what shotgun.

When the gun is discharged, the *firing pin* hits the back of the shell either on the center or on the rim (depending on whether the weapon is center-fire or rim-fire), marking it in a way that, like the marks of the rifling, is distinctive. Therefore it is almost always possible to say what rifle, revolver, pistol or shotgun fired what cartridge or shell.

What About Caliber and Gauge?

You've heard firearms described as .45-caliber, 12-gauge. If you're a hunter or if you've been in the military, you probably know what those terms mean. Otherwise, you don't. So here goes.

Gauge, which is used to measure only shotguns, has to do with the weight, in fractions of a pound, of what the shotgun would fire if it were firing solid ball ammunition instead of pellets. Thus, a 12-gauge shotgun would fire a solid ball of lead weighing 1/12 of a pound; a 10-gauge shotgun would fire a solid ball of lead weighing 1/10 of a pound. (I'd hesitate even to write about home-loading a shotgun shell this way. I'd be afraid somebody would try to do what I said and wind up blowing up the barrel, with probably fatal results.) Although theoretically this round ball of lead would exactly fit the barrel, I suspect the fit may be rather tight. The shotgun, remember, is not rifled. (It is possible to purchase rifled slugs for shotguns, but they are specially made.)

Shotgun shells are changing: Shotguns are customarily used for shooting wildfowl. There have been repeated incidents of ducks and geese dying by flocks from lead poisoning when lake levels dropped and the birds, instinctively seeking the small gravel they customarily have in their crops to allow them to digest their food, consumed lead shot left on the bottom of the lake. As a result, more and more shotgun shells are being made with safer steel shot instead of lead shot. Shotgun aficionados argue at great length as to whether the steel shot is better or worse than lead shot; what is certain is that it is lighter, and therefore steel shot needs to be about two shot sizes larger to have about the same shot pattern as lead shot. University of Utah student Joel Grose researched this situation in depth for a paper and reported that an ounce of number-six steel shot will have a considerably tighter shot pattern (that is, more pellets concentrated in a smaller area) than an ounce of number-six lead shot; in order to get the same shot pattern, number-four or even number-three steel shot would have to be substituted. (The number here pertains to a formula that calculates the number of pellets per ounce. For more detailed information, you might prefer to talk with the owner of a gun shop, as s/he can answer specific questions.)

Grose further pointed out that a shotgun, because of its smooth bore, cannot be at all accurate at over about fifty or fifty-five yards. These items of information might be useful in writing, particularly if your character is firing a shotgun using an old shell loaded with lead shot and then a new shell loaded with steel shot.

What does *caliber* mean? *Caliber*, which is used to describe weapons other than shotguns, has to do with the nominal diameter of the barrel (hence of the ammunition) expressed in hundredths of an inch; in real life, there are some discrepancies, but this is another of those areas I would not attempt to discuss in fiction without first talking with a gunsmith. Thus, a .38 revolver has a barrel .38-inch in diameter. A .30-caliber rifle fires bullets .30-inch in diameter. *Magnum* used in a description of a firearm refers not to the caliber but to the firepower of the propellant used; however, normally a magnum firearm is a slightly different caliber from the closest caliber of regular firearm—thus, you have .357 magnums which can fire .38 ammunition, but don't try to fire .357 magnum ammunition in a .38 revolver; it will fit the chamber and cylinder, but the firing mechanism and the barrel aren't meant to withstand a magnum load. However, .45-caliber ammunition cannot be used in a .44 magnum firearm at all, nor, of course, can .44 magnum ammo be used in a .45-caliber firearm. In general, it is *extremely dangerous* to attempt to fire anything in any firearm other than the ammunition designed to fit it. Even though in some cases ammunition may appear to fit, it may actually damage the barrel and/or firing chamber irreparably or even cause an explosion.

Some calibers of guns and ammunition, such as the 9mm, are

measured in millimeters rather than in inches. This measurement format, however, remains relatively uncommon in American-made civilian firearms, although it is frequently encountered in European-designed weaponry and in military firearms.

Sometimes, ammunition and the weapons that use that ammunition are described by a name that refers both to the caliber and to the year that specific type of ammunition was first used. .30-30 ammunition was first used in 1930; .30-06 (in speech, this is called *thirty-ought-six*) was first used in 1906. Where weapons seem to be the same caliber but the ammunition is not interchangeable, the difference usually has to do with such things as the overall length of the cartridge and/or the explosive force of the charge, as in the case of the .22 short, the .22 long, and the .22 long rifle ammunition, which in most but not all guns can be used interchangeably.

How can you tell whether any given ammo can be used in any given firearm? If the weapon is yours and you bought it new, the manufacturer's instructions will tell you. Otherwise, ask someone knowledgeable. By the time you're into that type of question, you've reached the point where you need a good reference book exclusively about firearms, or even better, a good gunsmith who will patiently answer questions.

The number of lands and grooves (which of course is identical, as each two lands are separated by a groove and each two grooves are separated by a land) and the direction of twist cannot possibly be addressed in this book; firearms examiners have immense reference books containing this information. Short tables for hundreds of the more common firearms appear in *American Ammunition and Ballistics* by Edward Matunas, which is listed in the bibliography. If it is not in your library, you can obtain a copy of it through interlibrary loan.

More Information Sources

Obviously, this is only the bare beginning of an outline about weapons. If you intend to get at all technical in your fiction, you would be well advised to buy several good reference books—at least one current one such as *The Shooter's Bible*, which appears annually, and at least one on historical firearms. Michael Newton's *Armed and Dangerous: A Writer's Guide to Weapons*, published by Writer's Digest Books, is especially useful, as it is designed for the writer rather than for the police officer or forensics technician.

Firearms at the Scene

What firearms evidence should be collected at the scene of the crime? What can be determined from what is collected?

Obviously, if a weapon is present, it must be collected and transported as gingerly as possible in hopes of preserving fingerprints. To handle a pistol or revolver, either lift it gingerly by the grips, or slide a pen or pencil, or a piece of string or wire, through the trigger guard *behind*—not in front of—the trigger, and lift it with that. When lifting it by the grips, carefully avoid touching the *backstrap*, the strip of metal separating the grips. A shoulder weapon is best lifted only after examining the weapon carefully and determining what part of this particular weapon is least likely to retain prints, because of checkering or repeated handling in exactly the same spot. (*Checkering* refers to a small, checkerboard effect carved into the surface to increase grip security.)

In real life, *Be careful! Always assume that any weapon is loaded unless you personally have verified that it is not! Every year many people are killed with "unloaded" firearms!* I've seen a few too many of those corpses to feel casual about the matter. In fiction, follow the needs of the plot—which may include substantial carelessness in handling and using weapons.

In general, it is difficult to get fingerprints from firearms, because the *stock* (the wooden, rubber or plastic part of shoulder weapons) and the *grips* (the wooden, bone or plastic handles of a pistol or revolver) are either too checkered or too often handled, or both, to yield prints. Further, the metal parts are generally too well-oiled or too often handled. However, I have gotten extremely good prints from firearms, so it's always worth trying. In fiction, you can decide whether to have prints, not to have prints, or to have prints that somebody stupidly damages.

Remember, always, that the weapon, like any other piece of evidence, should be photographed and triangulated before being moved. (This does not mean that somebody in your book can't stupidly—or deliberately—move the weapon without taking photos and measurements.)

The weapon must be handled very carefully for several reasons.

First, it may be still loaded, and it may have a hair trigger—that is, it may have been adjusted to discharge very easily. In fact, some shotguns will go off without anyone touching the trigger, if they are dropped or otherwise roughly handled. I worked two cases in which the victim—in one case, a twelve-year-old boy and in the other, the wife of a police sergeant—was killed with a shotgun nobody was even touching at the time. One of my cousins was seriously injured and one of my brothers narrowly escaped injury or death in two separate episodes of unintended keep-away played with a shotgun. (In both cases, the owner of the weapon was trying to get it back from a fraternal usurper.) That's something very useful in fiction, although in real life it should serve as a reminder that loaded guns should *never* be placed where children can get hold of them.

Also, it is important to preserve the evidential value of the weapon, which might include fingerprints on the outside of the weapon as well as the rifling inside the barrel and the marks on the firing pin.

It is essential to search for and collect any slugs that might be present at the scene, as when a slug missed or went through whoever it was aimed at. If it went through, the slug needs to be collected extremely carefully and put in a paper (not plastic) coin envelope, so that any moisture still on it can evaporate harmlessly. The lab might be able to locate microscopic fragments of cloth, bone or body tissue on it. If the slug has lodged in a wall or door frame, your detective *should not* try to dig it out. Instead, s/he should remove the entire section of wall or door frame and let the lab extricate the bullet. An ill-planned attempt to do the extrication may hopelessly damage the lands and grooves or other evidentiary markings.

If, as often happens, the slug lodged inside the victim's body, the medical examiner after the autopsy should, depending on the jurisdiction, turn the slug over to the investigating officer or directly over to the lab.

What Would Happen in Your Jurisdiction?

How do you know what would happen in your jurisdiction?

Ask the crime-scene technician. You may need to ask a public relations officer to introduce you to the crime-scene technician, but chances are the public relations officer himself or herself does not possess the crime-scene information you need.

While you're about it, find out whether your jurisdiction has a coroner only, a medical examiner only, or a coroner and a medical examiner. If it has a coroner, find out what his/her qualifications are. Many coroners are no more than funeral directors. You can do a lot in fiction with an incompetent coroner.

Things get more complicated if the shooting took place outside, or if (as sometimes happens) the slug went through a wall and exited outdoors. That's when it sometimes takes a careful search, using metal detectors if possible, to locate the slug. In that case, triangulation is especially important, as a line drawn from the final location of the slug through the hole in the wall can usually be extended to locate the exact spot from which the weapon was fired and, often, the height of the person who fired it as well.

Once that has been determined, experts can, if necessary, determine from what positions the muzzle flash should have been visible and from what places the report should have been audible. Although in real life this is rarely useful, in fiction it may be possible to locate a potential witness, or impeach a lying one, based on what has been determined from these tests. (I spent the better part of two years off and on trying to get a lead on a shooting that occurred in an alley, despite the fact that I was in the alley when the killing took place and didn't know about it until it was reported.)

Oh, you want to know more about that one? Well, it was this way. We—my husband and I—were in a mortgage company that backed onto the alley, arranging for a home loan. The back door of the mortgage company was open, and all three of us—my husband and I, as well as the agent we were talking with—heard the shot. We all got up, rushed back to the door, looked out into the alley, saw no sign whatever of any trouble, decided we had heard a backfire, and went back to the discussion in progress. I found out an hour later that the owner of a somewhat disreputable pawnshop, which was located in the alley and which sold musical instruments and repaired shoes on the side, had been shot to death—almost certainly by the shot we all heard.

Despite a lengthy and careful crime-scene investigation and a painstaking job of investigation by detectives, no suspect was ever developed. I have a few hunches of my own, as do the others who worked on the case, but none of them ended up proving anything.

How Far Can You Shoot?

Be aware, both in real life and in fiction, that a weapon may be able to fire farther than the person can see. Even a little .22 long rifle bullet (despite its name, it's as often used in pistols as in rifles) may travel as far as a mile, so that a person "popping cans" on a back fence in even a sparsely populated area may kill a person inside a house two blocks away. In November 1991, while I was working on this book, two young men got themselves into serious trouble on the Wasatch Front in Utah by setting up a firing range in their above-ground basement. When they began shooting at their targets with their .22s, their bullets passed out their wall and into the wall of the adjacent house, doing considerable damage. Fortunately, no one was seriously hurt, and the firing range was quickly discontinued.

In fiction as in real life, this carrying power means that the search for a slug — or the search for the place from which a weapon was fired, if it is known where the slug wound up — may occupy quite a large area.

Collecting and Using the Brass

In the case of an automatic or semiautomatic weapon, empty shells — usually referred to by police as *brass* — are ejected, and can be located unless the perp takes them away. Once located, the shells can be matched to the weapon (once the weapon has been located) by the firing pin mark on the shell and the ejector mark on the shell. Once again, photographing and triangulating are very important, as once the weapon is located, test firings that demonstrate how far, and in what direction, empties are ejected may — like triangulation of where the slug wound up — determine exactly where the person who fired the weapon was standing.

The empties should be collected very carefully. Albeit rarely, it has happened that a sufficiently large fragment of fingerprint for identification has been found on an ejected shell.

Ammo at the Scene

When searching a crime scene in which the perp probably lived in the house or in which the perp may have grabbed a weapon that was already in the house, it is critical to locate and collect every source of ammunition in that house, so that shells can, if possible, be matched to the source.

The Expert In–and Out of–the Lab

What can be determined, and by whom, about guns and ammunition?

- Firearms experts can usually–depending on the condition of the slug–determine what make, model and caliber of weapon fired any given slug.
- Firearms experts can usually–again depending on the condition of the slug–determine whether a suspect weapon fired any given slug.
- Firearms experts *cannot* usually determine which shotgun fired which load of shot.
- Almost always–except in the rare instances in which a shell has been reloaded and refired several times–firearms examiners can determine which weapon fired which empty shell. This refers to handguns, rifles and shotguns.
- Using a gunpowder residue test, forensic chemists can usually determine whether or not a given person fired a gun within the last few hours, provided the test is used quickly enough.

Firearm and Trace Metal Residue Tests

However, the old paraffin test, which was extremely inaccurate, has been totally discredited. Its technique of coating the hands with warm (not hot) molten paraffin, letting the paraffin harden, then stripping it off and checking it chemically for nitrates (the most common chemicals released when a gun is fired) not only gave false negatives when an insufficient quantity of gunpowder residue was present, it also gave false positives if the suspect had been working with fertilizer or even changing a baby's diaper.

The best test is a neutron activation analysis (NAA), but this test is so expensive that it is not always used. The test is done on swabs dipped in a 5 percent solution of nitric acid and wiped over the suspect's hands in a given order with particular concentration on the palms of the hands and the webbing between the thumb and first finger, where gunpowder residue tends to collect in the creases. The NAA tests for the less-common barium and antimony contained in gunpowder. Fortunately, the same chemicals and techniques used in the field for the NAA are also used for less expensive chemical tests, so the investigator does not have to decide at once which is to be used.

However, the better the weapon, the less powder it is likely to discharge onto the shooter's hands. A really well constructed weapon may produce a negative residue test unless an actual NAA is used, rather than its chemical stand-in; a Saturday night special may discharge so much powder that "powder tattooing" may be visible for several days on the webbing between the forefinger and the thumb. (It may also begin to shave lead after it's been fired several times. "Shaving lead" means that the barrel is so far out of line with the cylinder that although most of the slug goes out the barrel, a thin sliver of it is propelled backwards toward the shooter's hand. This happened to me once, when I was test-firing a cheap .22 pistol. The lead shaving produced a cut and the gunpowder got in the cut. I do not recommend this for fun.)

A trace metal test used quickly enough can almost always determine whether a particular person has *held* a firearm in the last twenty-four hours. This is a field test: the technician sprays a chemical from an aerosol can onto the suspect's hands and then examines the hands under black (ultraviolet) light. The hands then glow different colors according to what types, and shapes, of metals the person has handled recently. The test works because handling any metal results in the transfer of submicroscopic molecules of metal from the object to the person's hands, and the chemical is able to detect these molecules. In test situations, it has been possible to see the horse-head insignia from a Colt revolver on the hands of the person who held the revolver.

If both trace metal and gunpowder residue tests are to be performed, the trace metal test must be done first, as the nitric acid solution removes the metal molecules on which the trace metal test depends. Also, although a lot of soap and water may on occasion remove the gunpowder residue, they usually do not remove the metal molecules the trace metal detects. This means that in fiction you can do a lot with using only one test, or with using them in the wrong order, or with letting the suspect wash his hands thoroughly before running any tests.

In Real Life: A Murder That Wasn't

And here's how it once worked in real life.

Detective Johnny Patton went to a killing. It looked like a murder. The dead woman was sprawled in the middle of the floor; women almost always lie down to commit suicide. There was no suicide note; women almost always leave one. The wound, although very close range, was not contact. The pistol that had apparently killed her lay several feet away from her. The wound went in a slightly downward direction, as if she had been shot by someone taller than she was. She and her boyfriend had been involved in a crime, and they knew that they were facing arrest. The roof, in effect, had caved in on them.

Neighbors had heard the two quarreling loudly. Neighbors had seen the boyfriend leave suddenly. Nobody had heard the gunshot.

The boyfriend was the obvious suspect.

But for some reason he told me he couldn't define, the case didn't "smell" right to Johnny. There was no ident officer on duty. Johnny called me to come in.

I did a trace metal on the boyfriend's hands. He had not held a weapon.

I did a trace metal on the victim's hands. She had held a pistol, in normal suicide position.

I did gunpowder residues on both, and Johnny suspended the investigation until the results came back from the lab.

The victim had fired a pistol. The boyfriend had not.

As we reconstructed the crime, the victim had held the pistol at arm's length and slightly up to fire into her chest, letting the recoil throw the pistol away from her, simultaneously committing suicide and framing her boyfriend for her murder.

Was the frame job deliberate?

There was no proving it, of course, but Johnny and I always thought it was. And if Johnny hadn't been experienced enough, and good enough, to sense that something was wrong and call me in, the boyfriend might have been convicted. The evidence against him was strong enough that a negative firearms residue and trace metal on him might not have meant anything, if we hadn't also had a positive firearms residue and trace metal on the victim.

You may have the case if you want it . . . but I already sold a short story using the forensic part and the legal part, but not the human part, of the case.

TABLE 3
Some Characteristics of Handguns

- **Automatic pistol:** may be set for single shot usage, or may be set to go on firing as long as the trigger is depressed and ammunition remains in the magazine; each shot discharges a round of ammunition, ejects the empty, pulls another round into firing position, and—if it is set for full automatic, the trigger remains depressed, and ammunition remains in the magazine—fires again. When it is set for single shot usage, it works like a semiautomatic (see below).

    It is loaded by inserting a magazine, which may be loaded immediately before insertion or may have been loaded earlier. The number of shells in the magazine varies according to make and caliber; in combat situations, people usually carry extra loaded magazines.

    An automatic pistol generally has a safety mechanism to prevent accidental discharge.

    Examples: Beretta 9mm, Glock 9mm.

- **Semiautomatic pistol:** frequently referred to as an automatic, although it is not a full automatic because it cannot be set for continuous fire. Before it is fired the first time, a slide must be pulled back to bring the first bullet into firing position. When it is fired, the empty brass is ejected and another shell is pushed into firing position, but the trigger must be released and redepressed before it fires again.

    It loads with an insertable magazine, often called a *clip*. As in the case of an automatic, the magazine may be loaded immediately before insertion or earlier. The number of shells contained in a magazine varies according to make and caliber. The most common automatics have nine-shot clips, but some 9mm pistols on the street carry 30-round clips. In combat situations, people generally carry extra loaded clips.

    A semiautomatic pistol generally has a safety mechanism to prevent accidental discharge.

    Examples: U.S. Army Colt .45, Browning .22 target pistol.

- **Double-action revolver:** probably the most common handgun in civilian use today. It can be fired with a squeeze of the trigger; cocking is not necessary. Depressing the trigger automatically pulls the hammer back into cock position and then releases the hammer, causing the weapon to fire. The cylinder then rotates to bring another shell into firing position. The empty brass remains in the cylinder until the cylinder is opened and cleared for reloading.

To load a revolver, it is necessary to open the cylinder, either by rotating it out to the side or by opening the gun on a hinge so that the cylinder and barrel fold forward from the grips and firing mechanism, providing access to the back of the cylinder. The number of shells contained in a cylinder varies according to make and caliber, but the most common revolvers have six-shot cylinders. Despite the invention of various fast-loading devices, it still takes considerably longer to empty the brass and load six shots into a revolver than it does to pop out an empty clip and snap a full one into a semiautomatic. This is one of the many reasons why police departments tend now to replace revolvers with automatics.

A revolver does not have a safety mechanism. The device on the side of the gun that some people mistake for a safety is in fact a cylinder-release device.

Technically a revolver is not a pistol, although almost everyone calls revolvers pistols.

Examples: Colt or Smith and Wesson .38 service revolver, Dan Wesson .357 Magnum revolver.

- **Single-action revolver:** an older-style handgun than the double-action revolver, it cannot be fired without cocking. To fire, it is necessary to cock it first by pulling back the hammer manually, usually with the thumb. When the trigger is then depressed, the weapon fires, but the cylinder in most models does not rotate to bring another shell into firing position until the revolver is cocked again. The empty brass remains in the cylinder until the cylinder is opened and cleared for reloading.

  To load a revolver, depending on the make it may be necessary to open the loading-gate (located at the back of the cylinder on the left side), or to open the cylinder by rotating it out to the side or by opening the gun on a hinge so that the cylinder and barrel lean forward from the grips and firing mechanism, providing access to the back of the cylinder. Of course, any revolver may be loaded or unloaded by pulling the cylinder pin and removing the cylinder entirely, but this is rarely done. The number of shells contained in a cylinder varies according to make and caliber, but the most common revolvers had six-shot cylinders, so do not confuse single-action with single-shot. The "six-shooter" of the Old West (see below) was a single-action revolver.

A revolver does not have a safety mechanism. The device on the side of the gun that some people mistake for a safety is in fact a cylinder-release device.

Relatively few single-action revolvers are still manufactured. The few that are range in price from Texas Longhorn Arms's $1,500 (but they make it in any caliber you want) to Uberti's $350 for a Model 1873 .38 special or .357.

- Agatha Christie novels occasionally mention an "automatic revolver." The name baffles me. I finally concluded that either she meant a double-action revolver, or else she wasn't nearly as up on guns as she was on poisons.

- Handguns that have names are usually named for their manufacturers: e.g., Smith and Wesson, Dan Wesson. The caliber (muzzle diameter) is usually also mentioned in millimeters or hundredths of inches.

Some confusion has arisen in the case of the prolific gun designer John M. Browning. In Europe, automatic pistols are called brownings (small b); that is the word in Russian. The Browning Automatic Rifle (BAR) is named for him because he designed it and because it was manufactured by the Browning Arms Factory in Belgium. His most famous handgun, the military .45-caliber, was manufactured by the Colt Arms Works in Connecticut. The American military calls this weapon the Browning Pistol Model 1911; most of the public, however, speaks of it as a Colt .45. This is probably because the most remarkable handgun of the Wild West was a Colt .44 revolver. The equally renowned Winchester .44 was a repeating rifle.

To make NATO's forces more compatible, the Browning .45 manufactured by Colt has been replaced, in military usage, by the Browning 9mm manufactured by Beretta in Italy. Browning is considered the Leonardo da Vinci of firearms design; every manufacturer is eager to use his name.

F O U R

WORKING WITH FINGERPRINTS

The advantages of the finger-print system over the Bertillon and other methods of identification have become so well established that the former has now been universally adopted as the means of personal identification.

—Hans Gross,
Criminal Investigation

Don't worry, we'll get back to the Jackson Street Corpse, discussed in chapter one, eventually.

Although the American military service has begun DNA "fingerprinting" for positive identification of bodies that could not otherwise be identified, even DNA fingerprinting cannot totally replace real fingerprinting and its associated palm prints, toe prints, sole prints, lip prints and even ear prints, because these prints can be located in places that DNA cannot.

Fingerprints, fingerprints, how I love fingerprints! And always have. When I was a kid and my father was making model airplanes, I would always beg him to coat my fingertips with glue so that I could peel the glue off and examine the marks made by the ridges of my fingertips.

As an adult, I worked with fingerprints—as well as with all other details of both major crime-scene search and photography—the rape squad, and the police department speaker's bureau, for five and a half years in Albany, Georgia. Then I commanded the identification section of the Plano Police Department in Plano, Texas, for a year.

Within my first year in Albany, Captain Luther (head of ident) and I had taken about 10,000 unclassified, unused and misfiled fingerprint cards, classified them, invented a system for and drew up locator cards, created a general file and several special files (including a palm print file, a burglar file, and a sex-crimes file), and made idents (sometimes as many as twenty to twenty-five *nonsuspect* idents a month without a computer—a phenomenal record). We began requiring major case prints, which included palm prints and prints of the entire length and tips of all fingers and the sides of the palms, from all forgery, robbery and burglary suspects. I began to memorize some fingerprints I was particularly eager to locate (the FBI says that is impossible; I do not know their rationale for that assertion), and I made several nonsuspect idents from palm prints. (That, also, is impossible, according to the FBI, though their rationale on that one is clearer: Their files are too large to permit manual searching.) I cleared one robbery case—on a fingerprint I had memorized—a year to the day after the robbery took place.

What Holds Fingerprints?

This cannot possibly be all, but here are some things I know of that hold fingerprints: aluminum windowscreen frames, paper of all kinds, painted surfaces, unpainted wooden surfaces, live plants, tomatoes, Band-Aids, glass, copper pipe, human skin (if you're fast enough), galvanized metal, firearms, ejected brass from an automatic, shells left inside a revolver, automobile bodies, plastic, and the insides of rubber gloves left at the scene. With very thin gloves and hands with pronounced friction ridges, the prints may be left even through the gloves, a fact that badly confuses the perp when he finds himself arrested on fingerprint evidence after using gloves. There are some things you cannot get prints from: most undressed wooden surfaces (unless they're extremely smooth and previously unhandled), bricks, most rocks and stone, most cloth, most extremely dusty surfaces (although there is a new electrostatic process that makes lifting of prints made in dust possible, it is comparatively expensive and out of the financial reach of smaller departments).

In defense of my fellow identification technicians, I must hastily add that it is impossible to be able to count on *always* getting prints from *any* surface. There are too many variables, including the heat and humidity of the surrounding air, the cleanliness of the surface, and the condition of the hands of the person who left the prints. So for fictional purposes, you decide whether you want prints to have been left in this case or not.

How Long Do Fingerprints Last?

Again, there are many variables. On a hard surface, in cold, dry weather, the print may be gone almost instantly. On the same surface, in warm, humid weather, the print may last for weeks if it is undisturbed. On absorbent surfaces such as unglazed paper, the print is almost certainly there permanently; in an experiment, scientists using ninhydrin were able to locate the scribe's fingerprints on an ancient Egyptian papyrus.

And for an absolutely terrific scene of fingerprinting — definitely the best I ever saw in fiction — read Martin Cruz Smith's *Gorky Park*, the scene where detectives fingerprint the workshop that was making the fake antiques.

Fingerprints and the Jackson Street Corpse

Now let's get back to the Jackson Street Corpse. You still don't know who he is. And once again, you're Detective N.E. Boddy.

You've already taken care of the evidence outside the house, what little there was, because there was so little that once the photographs and measurements were made and the corpse was removed, there was nothing left to do outside. You've already taken the photographs and measurements inside. Now it's time to get to work with fingerprint powder and evidence bags.

Chain of Custody

Figure 4-1 is an evidence tag. All the information on it is absolutely critical; the last two-thirds of the tag consists of what is called the *chain of custody*. (You may remember that I mentioned chain of custody in chapter three, in reference to the Sacco-Vanzetti case.)

Without a complete chain of custody detailing in whose custody the evidence was at all times between the time it was collected and the time it was presented in court, the evidence becomes inadmissible — as it should. Although even a proper chain of custody does not

Date .... Time .... Case # ....

Location ....

Description ....

....

Collected by ....

Released to .... Date ....

Released to .... Date ....

Released to .... Date ....

Released to .... Date ....

Released to .... Date ....

Released to .... Date ....

Released to .... Date ....

Released to .... Date ....

Figure 4-1. Evidence tag.

totally prevent anyone from tampering with the evidence, it at least makes it possible to begin to find out who did the deed if evidence has been tampered with.

If the evidence is small enough to put in a bag, you'll use a special bag (either paper or plastic) that has an evidence tag printed on it. If the evidence is too large for that, you'll either tie or tape the evidence tag onto the evidence — but you won't do either of those until after you've fingerprinted the evidence; otherwise you might put the tag right where a fingerprint might be.

The blank card in Figure 4-2 is what you're going to put lifted latent fingerprints on, after you develop them with black powder. In common with any other evidence, the fingerprint lift must be very carefully labeled.

Now that you have your labels in order, it's time to start fingerprinting. How do you go about that?

The kit contains black powder, white powder, gray powder and red powder, often referred to as *dragon's blood* because it's a finely ground powder of dried sap of the dragon tree. When fingerprinting first began about ninety years ago, these powders were often made of lead—black lead, white lead, red lead, and a gray mixture of mercury and chalk. The mortality rate among early fingerprint technicians must have been terrific; unfortunately, no really adequate white or gray fingerprint powder other than white lead and the gray mercury mixture has ever been developed. So every kit contains nice, safe white and gray powders that virtually no fingerprint technician ever uses because they tend to fill between the ridges when used to develop latents; the fact is, almost all fingerprint technicians use the black powder almost exclusively. Although the vials of powder that fit inside a field kit hold only about two ounces, Doc Luther and I began after about a year to buy two-pound jars of powder and refill the field kits.

Dusting for Prints

The kits come with stiff brushes that I don't like because the bristles tend to cut the print. I prefer a very expensive, large, fluffy fiberglass brush. Here's the technique:

- First, examine the item with a flashlight, pointing the light in several different directions, as very often a *latent* (invisible until

Figure 4-2. Blank fingerprint lift card. It looks like a blank index card because very often that's exactly what it is.

developed) print is in fact *patent* (visible) under light coming from the appropriate angle.

- Then, twirl the handle of the brush between the palms of your hands to fluff out the bristles.
- Next, dip the very tip of the brush into the powder.
- Begin to brush the dust very lightly onto the print (or onto the item to be dusted, if light has not revealed a print).
- As soon as a print becomes visible, brush very carefully and lightly in the direction of the flow of the print.
- If necessary, blow excess powder off with your breath. Most of the time, the brush will take off the excess powder, but sometimes stray grains remain when more brushing might damage the print.
- Then, using special pressure-wound tape, press the tape very carefully, leaving no air pockets, down on the print.
- Using your thumb, forefinger or pencil eraser, press the tape down onto the print as hard as possible.
- Then, in *one motion*, because pausing will leave lines on the tape, lift the tape from the item.
- Press the tape down *on the edge* of a lifting card.
- Only then do you cut it from the roll, preferably with a sharp pocketknife.
- *Immediately*—not waiting till later because you will certainly forget even if you think you won't—label the lift card, note it in your notebook, and put the lift in a safe place.

Sometimes, if the print was still quite moist when you began working with it, you can make two or three lifts from the same dusting with increasing clarity each time. But if you do that, be prepared to explain in detail to the jury how and why you did it.

You may, if you read very old mysteries, have come across a description of people dusting for fingerprints with a gadget called an *insufflator*. I never saw one, but I have in my mind that it's sort of a cross between an ear syringe and a bulb-spray-type perfume atomizer. Suffice it to say, nobody uses them anymore.

You've started by dusting the door frame, just in case somebody you didn't know about was in the house that night. Now let's see how the lift is going to look, in Figure 4-3.

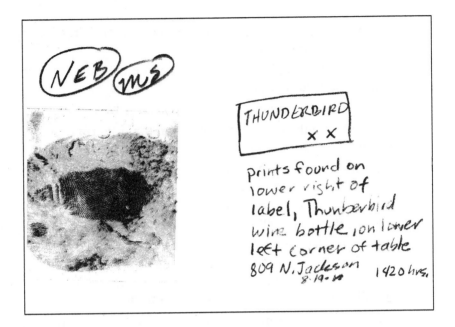

Figure 4-3. Lift card with lift on it. Notice that N.E. Boddy has drawn on the card a very rough sketch of where on the item the prints were found. Notice also that the lift itself is as close to the edge of the card as possible. This is for ease in working later, as well as for neatness.

Who initials those cards? Why, you, of course — Detective N.E. Boddy, and your partner, Mel(vin) or Mel(anie) Smith.

That's about the best you're going to be able to do on this surface; too many hands have been laid on top of hands for you to get anything more identifiable than a bowl of spaghetti. It's time to start on those seventeen liquor and wine bottles. If you just had one you might take it in and dust it in the office, but with seventeen, there's too much chance of bottles rolling against each other and breaking, or of prints being rubbed off by paper rubbing against the bottles. So you're going to do it all right now, right here.

Bottles can be tricky. The surface is so glossy that regular fingerprint brushes, even carefully used, tend to cut the print. You have something special to use on them: magnetic powder, so nothing except the powder itself will ever touch the surface being dusted. The "brush" is a wand containing a magnetic metal post inside a flexible closed rubber tube, and the fingerprint powder is extremely finely ground black iron filings. The wand can be held in either of two positions: with the metal post held up in the handle, so that the tube does not pick up fingerprint powder, or with the metal post pushed down into the tube, so that the tube does pick up the fingerprint powder. Theoretically, magnetic powder cannot be used on any surface that reacts to magnetism. But that, as you'll see later, is only theoretical.

All right, you've made several lifts from this bottle. You already know what the fingerprint lifting card looks like, so let's not bother with making more of them. Instead, let's go on and write up the evidence tag (see Figure 4-4), as you're going to want to take all the bottles that held prints into the police station with you.

Notice that once again, both you and Mel initialed the card, although only one of you collected the evidence. Notice also that each individual piece of evidence collected at any given crime scene will be given a separate item number, keyed to notes in the investigator's notebook. How many items might you collect at a crime scene? As few as zero, as many as thousands. How long does it take? It takes as long as it takes. There's no other possible answer. I spent two entire days working a crime scene inside an automobile, collecting several hundred pieces of evidence. As I recall, in the real Jackson Street Corpse case, I spent several hours there that afternoon.

It was a Saturday. I had been shopping, and I did not possess a pager. Police cars all over town were asked to look for me, and an

Date 08/19/~ Time 1445hrs Case # 18967
(see notebook)

Location on table, 809 N. Jackson

Description RedThunderbird wine bottle,
Item # 14 (see notebook)

Collected by (NEB) (ms)

Released to .... Date ....

Released to .... Date ....

Released to .... Date ....

Released to .... Date ....

Released to .... Date ....

Released to .... Date ....

Released to .... Date ....

Released to .... Date ....

Figure 4-4. Evidence tag.

officer spotted my car in the parking lot of a local department store and went in to haul me away from a going-out-of-business sale. I had my younger daughter, then not quite a year old, with me; she still remembers waiting in the car (a police officer played with her while I worked the crime scene) and then being dropped off at the day-care center long enough for me to wash my hair in the dark-room.

I went back again for several hours on Sunday and again on Monday, before I was to the point I could call myself through at the scene. How well I yet remember—I had ident all to myself then; it was before we had added a third person. Doc went on vacation to Florida, and the last thing he said to me before he left was, "I hope you have a corpse a day while I'm gone." He meant it as a joke; we'd never had that many in that short a period. (Doc's vacation lasted thirteen days. I had nine corpses, starting out Friday at 4:30 P.M. with a triple shotgunning where several innocent bystanders got in the way of a drug deal that went sour.)

But the murder rate increased steadily. The first year I was with the Albany Police Department, we had four murders the entire year. The last year I was there, we had four murders before New Year's Day was over.

More About Collecting Latents

Let's move on now to some more general methods of collecting latent prints, and look at a few more specific examples of those methods in use. Bear in mind that we're still talking about collecting latents; we'll get on to fingerprinting people (alive or dead) a little later.

There are four main ways of collecting latents:

- Dusting
- Spraying
- Dipping
- Fuming.

Dusting is the most common. You've already looked at dusting with a regular brush and with magnetic powder. In general, magnetic powder is never used on magnetic objects; that is, it is not used on steel, iron, or any other object that has any built-in magnetic property of its own. But that generalization, like most generalizations, is not true in some specific cases. And therein lies a tale. I remember it well. So does the Georgia Supreme Court, to which it was appealed.

How the Georgia Supreme Court Ruled Me Expert

A small mom-and-pop grocery store was robbed. I was busy on something else; I didn't get the original call. Detective Howard Yelverton got there soon after the uniform officers did, and because the perp had definitely fled on foot, Howard called for the dogs.

Bear in mind that you must use specially trained dogs to find a scent trail, although bloodhounds are not required. In Albany, Georgia, when we needed dogs we borrowed them from the nearby Lee County Prison Branch. The dogs—actually one dog, a well-trained German shepherd—arrived in a truck. His trainer showed him where the trail had started, and he took off through yards and back alleys. A couple of blocks away, he stopped at a house and began barking lustily—nowhere near a door. In fact, he was standing by a back wall jumping up and down and barking.

The trainer took a look and called Howard, who was following a few paces behind the dog. Howard took a look, reached for his hand radio, and called me.

By the time I arrived, the dogs were gone. But the television cameras were still there, and the television news later showed a picture I could really have done without: me from the back, leaning over, very carefully collecting the shiny bright chrome-plated .38 revolver that the perp—whoever he was—had stopped long enough to drop behind a loose board.

The people in the store said their assailant had been very careful about prints; he'd wiped with his shirttail everything he touched. Evidently he did that with the revolver, too. He very, very carefully wiped off, with his shirttail, every fingerprint he'd left on the revolver until that moment—and then, equally carefully, he took the revolver in his hand, leaned over, and placed it inside the wall behind the loose board—leaving behind probably the best thumbprint I had ever seen in my life. Because of the angle of the sun, Howard saw the print as soon as he saw the gun.

As the detective and the television news team went on after dogs and dog trainer who were on the perp's trail, I rushed into the police station. I had a bit of a problem. Although the print was visible, and gorgeous, I had to get powder on it and lift it before I could begin to search it—that is, to find out whose print it was. And chrome is an extremely hard and glossy surface; powder and brushes, even the finest powder (which isn't fingerprint powder at all, but powdered photocopier toner) and the softest brushes tend to cut prints on chrome.

I had a good print on one side of the revolver. Turning to the other side, I made several test prints of my own thumb and then methodically began to try out different powders and brushes. Lo and behold, the mag powder—which is supposed to be unusable on any magnetic surface—worked beautifully on the chrome-plated steel. Turning the revolver over, I dusted and lifted the print. Then I headed for that collection of 10,000 fingerprint cards and started searching.

I knew that I had a thumb. I knew which hand it was from. I knew the pattern on that thumb. That narrowed the search down to less than 2,000 cards. But just for the heck of it, before I started searching the whole file, I searched the cards that were already on my desk.

And there it was. He'd been arrested for public intoxication less than two weeks before, and I still hadn't finished classifying and filing his card.

By the time dogs and police hauled Leon McCoy out of the house he had holed up in, I had his fingerprint card out with the latent lift paperclipped to it.

Yes, this time I'm using the perp's real name. After the kind of publicity that one got, there wouldn't be much sense in trying to disguise it.

Why the appeal?

The first trial was declared a mistrial. For the second trial, nobody could find the fingerprints and charts. The court thought I had them, and I thought the court had them. (They turned up, years later, in somebody else's file. To this day nobody knows how they got there.) Leon McCoy said: (1) I wasn't a fingerprint expert; (2) it was improper to base a conviction on fingerprints nobody could find; and (3) we were persecuting him because he was a Muslim.

The court ruled: (1) I was a fingerprint expert; (2) although normally the prints had to be produced, this was an unusual situation and the prints had been seen by enough people that the court decided their discussion, without their production, was proper; and (3) nobody but Leon McCoy seemed to care that Leon McCoy was a Muslim. (In fact, the local imam had in effect disowned him, and it was perfectly obvious why. Proper Muslims do not become intoxicated, in or out of a public place, nor do they go about robbing stores and then trying to get away with the crime on the basis of religion. Islam was at that time working very hard to be accepted in Georgia as a proper religion, and Leon McCoy wasn't helping much.)

I will add that of all the criminals who, after conviction, have ever promised to "git" me, Leon McCoy is about the only one I think is crazy enough to try. But it was still an interesting case. If you want to read more about it, it's *Leon McCoy v. The State of Georgia.* My name then was Martha G. Webb. (Never mind how I turned into Anne Wingate. That's another story entirely.)

Finding Latents on Paper

In general, paper is fumed or sprayed. But highly glazed paper, such as that found in high-quality magazines, is best treated by powders. In one case, the home of an FBI agent was burglarized. On the back of the FBI magazine found on the agent's nightstand was an enlarged photograph of an extremely interesting fingerprint—and fingerprint technicians dusting the glazed magazine cover found the fingerprint of the burglar on the photograph of the fingerprint.

Spraying is probably the second most common means of testing for latents; on paper, it is the most common. A chemical called ninhydrin is the most widely used spray; its chemical name is triketo-hydrindine hydrate. Ninhydrin, available commercially in an acetone solution, has an extremely strong and unpleasant metallic odor; many technicians also dissolve it in amyl acetate—which gives it the smell of slightly overripe bananas—because some inks run, and some fabrics dissolve, in an acetone solution. However, the acetone is much safer; too much amyl acetate causes severe headaches . . . and herein lies a story.

How not to develop prints on paper and cardboard: The Albany ident section eventually grew to three people. The third was Robert "Butch" Windham. Although he'd entered the police department about the same time I did, he was far less experienced with fingerprints, and he was noticeably hardheaded. When we began using ninhydrin dissolved in amyl acetate, we all knew of its headache-causing properties, and Doc warned us that if we were going to spray more than one or two items we should take them out in the open air to spray.

One evening, on duty by himself, Butch decided to spray a large number of cardboard boxes. He took them out in the open air, all right — directly under the intake for the police department's air-conditioning system. By the time he got through, the building had been evacuated and the entire on-duty dispatch section was in the hospital. One dispatcher, who was several months pregnant, never did return to work. She was not harmed, but she was extremely frightened.

How to develop prints on paper and cardboard: Although ninhydrin was developed in the nineteenth century as a specific reagent for amino acids, it was not applied to fingerprinting until 1954. Before that, iodine fuming and silver nitrate solutions were used to develop prints on paper. But iodine fumes are difficult to work with and extremely caustic, and silver nitrate, if not carefully controlled, will blacken the entire document.

When all three are to be applied, they must be used in this order:

- Iodine fuming
- Ninhydrin
- Silver nitrate (which may be sprayed or put in a dish for the document to be dipped in it).

However, most police departments use only ninhydrin. I have very rarely used iodine and never have used silver nitrate.

But iodine is essential in some espionage and other cases in which a document must be examined for fingerprints and then sent to its intended recipient, because almost always, iodine prints can be photographed and then treated with ammonia vapor so that they will completely fade out; in fact, they may fade out in the air unless they are sprayed with a fixative solution. Ninhydrin and silver nitrate are generally permanent, although manufacturers recommend fixing them also. (Both tend to be permanent on hands as well as on documents. Fingerprint examiners sometimes have very odd-looking hands. I suspect our lungs are pretty odd-looking as well; a fingerprint technician has to be totally away from work for more than two weeks before s/he quits sneezing fingerprint powder.)

Ninhydrin, as I mentioned, produces an unpleasant, acrid odor; however, as many as 50 percent or more of all fingerprint cases taken to court now involve fingerprints on paper, and at least 90 percent of those prints are developed with ninhydrin.

At times our lab resembled a laundry, with dozens of forged checks hung up on several small drying lines. It looked even funnier at the developing stage, when we started blowing the checks with a hair dryer.

Methods of Iodine Fuming

Prints developed with iodine are brownish-violet. Iodine fumes must be used inside a container; although commercial fuming tanks are available, an old glass fish tank with a light bulb in it to provide the heat to vaporize the iodine crystals is generally adequate. A sort of blowpipe, in which the technician's breath is blown through a fiberglass filter and over a handful of iodine crystals onto the paper, may be substituted. The paper must be watched carefully, as the prints develop quickly. The prints must then be photographed immediately, as unfixed prints will fade out almost as soon as they are removed from the iodine vapor. (Technicians use a special fingerprint camera, which produces a 1:1 ratio of negative to original—that is, a negative the same size as the original.)

Iodine works on oils from the skin surfaces that are transferred to the paper. (Fingertips do not produce oils; however, people touch their faces far more frequently than anybody but ident people realize, and oils from the face are transferred to the fingertips and hence to the paper.)

Methods of Using Ninhydrin

Ninhydrin is available in aerosol spray cans dissolved in acetone. Large-scale users can obtain it in crystal form; it is soluble in acetone or amyl acetate, and can be sprayed from plastic jars that use plain air rather than aerosol solutions as the propellant. The jars are slightly less efficient than the spray cans, but they are somewhat less expensive and probably safer for the environment. Dipping a document in ninhydrin dissolved in acetone is more efficient than spray cans or bottles, but it is also more likely to cause the ink to run. The spray form of this solution will not cause headaches, but if too much is sprayed in a small unventilated space, the user can wind up with chemical pneumonia. (I know. I did.)

Dipping a document in ninhydrin dissolved in amyl acetate will not cause the ink to run, and it is more efficient than using sprays, but it is far more likely to cause very severe headaches.

All of this means that each time ninhydrin is used, the user has to mentally weigh cost, efficiency, the need to keep the ink from running, and the possible health problems. These are all things you can use in fiction, especially if you're writing about a small department or a P.I. with a limited budget.

The prints developed with ninhydrin—which works on the amino acids contained in all perspiration—range in color from pink to purple. They develop in about twenty-four hours after the paper is sprayed, although some may continue to become visible for up to forty-eight hours after that. The stronger prints develop far more quickly under conditions of heat and moisture; we tried ironing them with a dry iron and with a steam iron, and later switched to the hair dryer, which worked very well.

However, one time we examined a check for the postal inspector and found no usable prints on it. The inspector then picked it back up from us and mailed it to the Postal Inspection Service Laboratory in Washington, D.C. Somewhere between our office and theirs the prints developed, so that when the check (properly packaged in a plastic sleeve so that no additional prints would be put on it) was removed from the envelope, the prints were quite clear.

Silver Nitrate in Developing

Silver nitrate, which reacts with the salt present in perspiration and hence in fingerprints, is used by dipping the paper in a silver nitrate solution or spraying the solution onto the paper. The paper is then exposed to normal light. It must then be watched extremely carefully, as it can go from clear black prints to entirely black paper in seconds. Once the prints have developed, the paper with the solution on it must be stored in absolute darkness, as every exposure to light recommences the darkening. Even paper that has been treated with a fixative will darken, although the darkening will be somewhat slower.

Other Methods of Fuming for Prints

Most people incorrectly believe that anything except paper is fingerprinted only with powder. Many other items, such as some plastics and all galvanized metal, are best treated by fuming. But these fumes don't come in a can. When I went through fingerprint school, I was told to burn a magnesium strip, which burns very quickly with a bright white flame and produces white smoke, to fume plastics and galvanized metal. Doc and I tried that exactly once and almost burned down the ident lab. We preferred fat pine (pine kindling wood), which produces a dense black smoke that liberally coats the item held above it. After the item has cooled, the excess smoke is brushed off with a normal fingerprint brush. There is no danger of brushing out these prints: The smoke actually fuses the print to the metal, and it's there forever. Sometimes, in multiple thefts from soft-drink machines, we got the coin boxes back to smoke two or three times and it got hard to tell which were the old prints and which were the new ones.

Fuming With Super Glue

The preferred fuming method now involves Super Glue. Yes, that's a trademarked product, and to start with that specific product was what we used. Since then, other products have been developed that work similarly, but most of the time, when a fingerprint technician says Super Glue, s/he means Super Glue. The glue is put onto a hard, nonflammable surface, and the item to be fumed is put near it. Then both are sealed into an airtight container. The prints, thick white in color, develop naturally in about forty-eight hours.

If more speed is needed, there are several methods of accelerating the process. One involves putting cotton balls soaked in sodium hydroxide near the Super Glue; another involves heating the Super Glue to about 200° Fahrenheit; and a third involves substituting a gel called Hard Evidence—a cyanoacrylate ester in a reusable sealed pouch—for the Super Glue. All have their advantages and disadvantages. Not only is Super Glue less pleasant to smell than fat pine, but also its use in this manner—which is *not* what the manufacturer recommends—can produce highly toxic fumes.

But it works on some extremely difficult surfaces. Probably there is no surface more difficult to fingerprint than a thin plastic bag, and Constable Garry Birch of Perth, Western Australia, was once faced with the task of printing 1,800 plastic bags that had been collected in a major drug raid. After some consideration, Birch acquired a large wooden crate used for overseas shipping. He then suspended the bags on strings draped across the container. He bought ninety-six tubes of glue and squeezed the glue onto three strips of aluminum foil, which he put on the bottom of the container. He then sealed the container for seventy-two hours.

Suspecting that much glue might have produced fumes nobody wanted to smell, he asked the fire department to open the container while using full breathing apparatus. After the fumes had dissipated, he examined the bags and found fingerprints on thirty of them.

Seventy-two hours may seem like a long time to wait for results. But if Birch had tried to dust with magnetic powder or photocopier toner, the only other reliable means of getting prints from thin plastic bags, he'd probably have spent a lot more time and might well have gotten worse results.

Technicians Steve Rowley and Bob Braman, in Salt Lake City, once Super Glue-fumed an entire airplane. Another technician, telling me about it, emphasized, "It wasn't a real airplane; it was only a Piper Cub." I assured him that I consider a Piper Cub a real airplane — especially for this purpose.

Lasers and X Rays

Less common methods of looking for latents include lasers and soft-tissue X rays. The FBI first used lasers in examining for prints on highly difficult items, such as the inside of powdered rubber gloves (yes, that's what I mean: the gloves were coated inside with powder before wearing) and the sticky side of tape, in 1980. In that year alone, they located 215 prints by that method, which led to forty-five convictions.

The Tokyo Police Department pioneered in the use of soft-tissue X ray to get fingerprints of a perp from the skin of a victim. This complicated method is still not available to most police departments because of the narrow time window in which such prints can be obtained and the lack of equipment; in fact, I am not familiar with any department that routinely uses this method. But that does not mean that your super P.I. can't use it.

More common — though still quite rare — means of getting prints from the victim's skin involve either thin silver plates or unexposed, developed, fixed, high-gloss, resin-coated photographic paper. Remember that as recently as twenty years ago, technicians believed that it was impossible to get prints from the victim's skin — although the materials with which this work is now done were already available.

Latents From Human Skin

Thin silver plates are given an extremely high polish using jeweler's rouge; the photographic print paper is cut into usable sizes, and then both are used approximately the same way. Both require several factors:

1. The victim's skin containing the print must be relatively dry and hairless. Hairy areas or moist, sweaty areas will not hold prints. Usually the only areas meeting this description are breast or abdomen skin or the inside of the wrist and upper arm.

2. The perp's hands must have been fairly moist, and must have well-developed ridges.

3. Minimal time must have passed. Twelve hours is about the absolute maximum if there is to be any chance of success.

The silver plate or the photographic paper is clapped down firmly, *in one motion*, on the victim's skin where s/he remembers having been touched. It is lifted off—again in one firm motion—and carefully dusted. In the case of the photographic paper, the developed latent is then covered with tape. However, this procedure produces the mirror image of a print lifted in the normal manner.

The silver plate is used the same way. When the print is transferred to a lifting card, it will produce a mirror image of a normal print. In order to work with either comfortably, you will need to make a photographic negative and then an internegative and then use the internegative the way you would normally use a fingerprint lift. See Figure 4-5 for an explanation.

In general, photographic paper is just as efficient and is far cheaper and easier to work with. According to the Tokyo Police Department, the soft tissue X ray provides better results. Unfortunately, as I said, it simply is not generally available in the United States. Your supercop can use it if s/he wants to.

Where to Look for Prints

Ident people spend a lot of time watching the way people use their hands. Notice, next time you are writing, the way your palm and little finger curl into a reverse C—or into a C, if you're left-handed—and rest on the paper. Those are the parts of the hand that leave prints on a forged check. Next time you start to drive an unfamiliar car, notice how you automatically adjust the rearview mirror. That's the best place to find prints in a stolen car—not the steering wheel,

 Fingerprint as it appears on victim's skin.

 **Silver plate:** Print not in normal lift position cannot be handled.

 **Internegative:** Print in normal lift position, can be handled but photo will be mirror image of normal lift position.

 **Negative:** Print in mirror image of normal lift position, so that photo will appear normal.

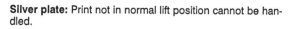 **Photo print:** Normal lift position.

Figure 4-5. Using the silver plate method for developing a latent from human skin.

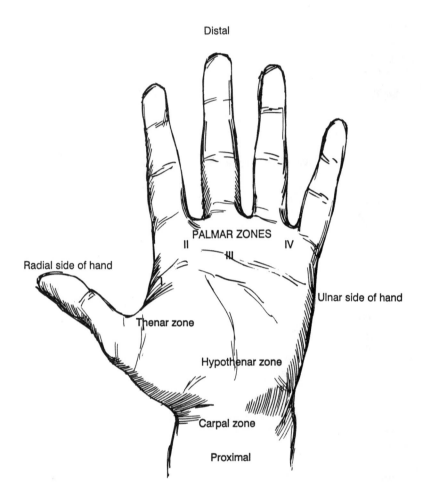

Figure 4-6. Nomenclature of the hand. Illustration by Tom Post.

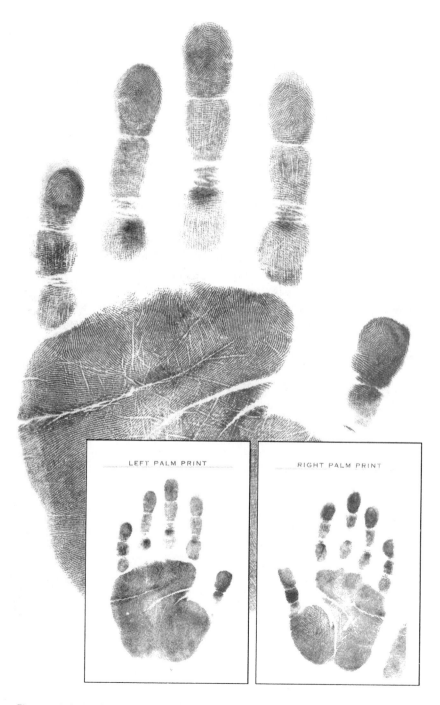

Figure 4-7. A standard palm print. The inset boxes show sample palm print cards.

on which the prints pile up on top of each other until they're totally illegible.

Figure 4-6 gives the names of the parts of the hands. The *thenar zone* and the *hypothenar zone* turn up most often on documents, especially on the backs of checks. The *palmar zone*, which is divided into several numbered areas for ease in discussion, turns up when something has been grasped. The thumb and the first three fingers turn up on opposite sides of something that has been grasped with the fingers rather than with the whole hand. The little finger almost never is found in crime scenes.

The *interpalmar zones* show up in various situations; again, the best way to figure out where to look for what, is the same way ident people do it: Watch the way people use their hands. If you are trying to decide for fiction what part of the hand would leave prints, actually put your hands through the actions your fictitious perp would have used. (This is done very well on "Murder, She Wrote." I've enjoyed watching Angela Lansbury twisting her hands around, regarding them with wide-mouthed and wide-eyed calculation.)

How Do You Know What You've Found?

I told you I knew that print on what turned out to be Leon McCoy's revolver was a thumb print as soon as I saw it. How did I know? How do you work with those prints from crime scenes?

We need another chapter for that.

TABLE 4

The Latent Fingerprint

These pages come from The Finger Print Manual, *published by Sirchie Finger Print Laboratories, Inc., and are used by permission. The charts have been edited for use in this publication.*

Latent fingerprints generally consist of a mixture of natural secretions from glands in the skin. Often these latent prints contain contaminants that are picked up on the skin (some fingerprints consist solely of contaminants).

Determination of the major constituents of a fingerprint by simple visual examination is usually impossible, unless the fingerprint is in an obvious contaminant (blood, grease, dust, etc.).

Distribution of the major constituents of secretions of the sweat glands and the actual distribution within a given latent fingerprint vary from donor to donor, and can greatly vary with the same donor at any given time (large variations occurring from day to day and even minute to minute).

Sweat Gland Secretion

There are three major sweat glands found in the human body: the eccrine glands, the sebaceous glands and the apocrine glands. The secretions of these glands are as follows:

Gland	Inorganic Compounds	Organic Constituents
Eccrine glands*	Chlorides Metal ions Ammonia Sulphate Phosphate	Amino acids Urea Lactic acids Sugars Creatinine Choline Uric acid
Sebaceous glands	—	Fatty acids Glycerides Hydrocarbons Alcohols

*The eccrine glands secrete a large amount of water in addition to the listed constituents.

Gland	Inorganic Compounds	Organic Constituents
Apocrine glands	Iron	Proteins Carbohydrates Cholesterol

Most natural fingerprints consist of a mixture of sebaceous and eccrine sweat. Some of these chemicals persist for long periods of time in latent fingerprints while others may decompose, evaporate or diffuse.

The presence of a specific chemical in a fingerprint depends on the constituents of the original fingerprint, the nature of the surface, the time elapsed since deposition, and the storage conditions. Factors such as temperature, exposure to light and water and the relative humidity affect the chemical and physical nature of a fingerprint.

Water is the first component to be lost from most fingerprints. Because of this, when dealing with prints more than a few days old, processes which primarily detect water are less effective than those processes which detect primarily the fatty component.

Detection of Latent Fingerprint Constituents

Some fingerprint detection processes are specific to particular chemicals, while others detect the oily or greasy physical nature of the surface.

Since the chemical and physical nature of a fingerprint is generally not known before the fingerprint examination, the techniques used and the order in which they are applied are determined primarily by the particular surface type the fingerprints are on.

Sebaceous (Fatty) Material	Eccrine (Aqueous) Material
Visual examination Powders Small particle reagent Fluorescence examination Iodine	Visual examination Powders Ninhydrin Cyanoacrylate (Super Glue) Silver nitrate Fluorescence examination

Methods for Latent Fingerprint Development

Powders: Many powders for the development of latent fingerprints are available. With fresh fingerprints, the aqueous component of the fingerprint contributes significantly to the adhesion of powders, while with older prints, powders adhere principally to the fatty deposits of sebaceous sweat. In many cases, flake powders such as Silver Latent Print Powder are more sensitive than other types of powder. In some instances, a less sensitive powder may be more effective.

Fluorescence examination: Some of the natural constituents and some types of environmental contamination found in latent prints will fluoresce under ultraviolet illumination. Treatments are available that cause fingerprints to fluoresce more strongly. Also, some types of fingerprints can be enhanced by using ultraviolet illumination that is absorbed by the fingerprint that excites the fluorescence of the background. (Ninhydrin-developed fingerprints are an example of this.)

Iodine: This technique is very simple to use. Iodine vapor is absorbed by latent fingerprint deposits (along with some reaction to unsaturated fats contained in the fingerprint) forming a brown image. The developed print should then be fixed to avoid any possible fading.

Ninhydrin: Ninhydrin is a general-purpose fingerprint reagent for paper and other porous surfaces. It reacts with amino acids in fingerprints. An intermediate colored image varying from orange to purple (depending on donor and conditions) is produced. With full development, the compound Ruhemann's Purple is produced. Full development can take several days, but the reaction can be accelerated by heating and humidification.

Silver nitrate: Silver nitrate can be used on raw wood surfaces. (Ninhydrin is preferred for use on paper.) Silver nitrate reacts with the chlorides contained in latent fingerprints producing silver chloride, which when exposed to light turns a dark gray.

Small particle reagent: This process is quick and simple. Small particle reagent is a suspension of fine molybdenum disulfide particles. Small particle reagent adheres to the fatty constituents of latent fingerprints to form a gray deposit. The developed print can be lifted to simplify photography.

Cyanoacrylate (Super Glue): Cyanoacrylate vapor develops fingerprints on a wide range of surfaces. The cyanoacrylate vapor produces a white deposit as a result of polymerization with the latent fingerprint. Water acts as a catalyst for this polymerization.

Smooth, nonporous: This includes such surfaces as glass, paint, varnish and hard plastic moldings. (Metals are not included.) Powders can be used effectively on most of these surfaces. Fluorescence examination, small particle reagent and cyanoacrylate can also be used on these surfaces.

Rough, nonporous: Rough or grained plastic moldings are examples of this surface type. These surfaces are generally unsuitable for effective use of powders; therefore, more success can generally be expected with small particle reagent and cyanoacrylate fuming.

Paper and cardboard: Paper and cardboard (including plaster board) that has not been waxed or plastic coated should be treated with ninhydrin. Powders may be used on smooth surfaces prior to treatment with ninhydrin, but powders are generally insensitive to older fingerprints.

Plastic packaging material: This includes such surfaces as polyethylene, polypropylene, cellulose acetate and laminated paper. Small particle reagent, cyanoacrylate and powders may be used, small particle reagent being very effective in many cases.

Soft vinyl (PVC), rubber and leather: Simulated leather and cling film are examples of these surface types. Small particle reagent, cyanoacrylate and powders may be used on these surfaces.

Metal (untreated): This applies to bare metal surfaces, not surfaces that have been painted or lacquered. Small particle reagent, applicable powder types and cyanoacrylate can be used on this type of surface.

Raw wood (untreated): Bare wooden surfaces that have not been painted or treated should be treated with ninhydrin. Smooth wood may be treated with powders, while silver nitrate may be used on light woods.

Wax and waxed surfaces: Articles made of wax (such as candles) and paper, cardboard and wood that have been coated with wax can be treated by nonmetallic powders and cyanoacrylate.

F I V E
MORE ABOUT FINGERPRINTS

Recent inventions make it possible now to send a "picture telegram"
between places at which perfectly synchronized instruments have been
installed. . . . There seems little doubt that as the technique of wireless
telegraphy develops, it will be possible to send natural-size photographs
of finger-prints by wireless for any distance.

—Hans Gross,
Criminal Investigation

That was written in 1934. But even I can remember a time when it
was essential to get a set of fingerprints from Georgia to Washington, D.C., in a matter of hours. We—the police officers and the
FBI—ran all over town until the FBI managed to locate somebody
who had a fax machine. I had to make separate 8 × 10 photo enlargements of each of the ten fingerprints, which took about two hours.
It took about ten minutes per enlargement to fax them—almost
another two hours. That was less than twenty years ago. Now, almost
every police department has a fax machine, and the card itself could
be faxed in less than twenty seconds.

But what are fingerprints? Where did the idea come from?

A Brief History of Fingerprinting

The first mention of fingerprints in Western fiction came, about the
same time, on both sides of the Atlantic: in stories by Mark Twain
(*Life on the Mississippi*) and Arthur Conan Doyle ("The Adventure

of the Norwood Builder"). The first recorded use of fingerprints that has been found so far—and we don't know whether it was for identification or for magic—came in a Babylonian text of about four thousand years ago, when several army deserters were recaptured and compelled to leave the marks of their fingers and thumbs. Although it would be more logical to assume that this was for some sort of magical purpose, the presence in archaeological excavations of well-designed magnifying lenses makes it at least possible that prints were being used for identification.

We're on surer ground by the time we get to China, about two thousand years ago: People were using their thumb marks as seals, and captured river pirates a thousand years ago were compelled both in fact and in fiction to provide ink prints of their thumbs. This thousand-year continuity provides strong evidence that the prints were being used for identification. Japan also has a strong history of the use of thumbprints as personal signatures and seals.

Fingerprints were first used in a criminal case in Rome in the time of the Caesars, although the size and shape of the prints were in question rather than the ridge detail. A senator was found murdered. His young second wife, hysterical, pointed to the bloody handprints on the wall near the murder, insisting that her blind stepson had committed the murder and then had to fumble his way from the body. The Praetorian Guard arrested the youth, who maintained his innocence. In court, his defense attorney was able to prove that the handprints were much too small to fit the young man, and that in fact the wife had committed the murder and deliberately made the prints in order to direct suspicion toward her husband's son from his first marriage.

The first known Western movement toward the use of fingerprints for identification occurred in Germany, in 1788, when J.C.A. Mayer stated that the skin ridges in two or more individuals are never identical. In 1856, also in Germany, Herman Welcker made a print of his right palm and stored it away. In 1897, he repeated the print and studied the two carefully, determining that there were no changes. Prior to that, in 1823, Professor Johannes E. Purkinje classified fingerprints, but he seems not to have realized that the prints were unchangeable and never identical from individual to individual.

Things came together at the end of the nineteenth century with the work of William Herschel in India, Henry Faulds in Japan, and

Francis Galton in England in 1892. Although Herschel and Faulds both noticed the individuality of fingerprints and used them for identification purposes, it was Galton who proposed a practical system of classification and filing. Sir Edward Richard Henry in 1899 and 1900 modified and improved upon Galton's system, enabling it to handle much larger files than Galton ever envisioned. Henry's system is still in use today in all of the English-speaking world and many other countries.

At virtually the same time, in 1891 in Argentina, Juan Vucetich was producing a system of fingerprint classification that is in use in most Spanish-speaking countries. Vucetich made the first known use of real fingerprints in a criminal investigation of the case of a woman who murdered her illegitimate children and tried to place the blame on her estranged boyfriend, who was not the father of the children. People who have used both the Vucetich system and the Henry system maintain that for anyone starting from scratch, the Vucetich system is far easier to learn. However, the Henry system is too deeply ingrained in most of the rest of the world to be easily changed now.

Interpol, of course, is able to work with both the Vucetich and the Henry systems; however, it is not an actual police agency but rather an international clearinghouse of police information. It has no jurisdiction or arrest powers of its own.

And how did fingerprinting reach the United States? In 1902, Dr. H.P. de Forest was able to require its use in the New York State Civil Service Commission, to cut down on fraud in the taking of tests. In 1904, during a world's fair in St. Louis, Missouri, a Scotland Yard inspector taught fingerprinting to several police officers in the United States. The entire U.S. armed forces had taken up fingerprinting by 1908.

The Will West Case

The value of the fingerprint system was conclusively proven in Leavenworth Federal Penitentiary in 1903. A prisoner was brought in by the name of Will West. Admission personnel, photographing and measuring him, insisted he had been there before, but he insisted he had not, and his conviction listed him as a first offender. His Bertillon measurements (see sidebar) and photographs seemed identical to those already on record for William West. But on further checking, personnel found that this could not be William West—because William West was still in prison!

When the two men were placed side by side, they looked like identical twins. But despite theories expressed even today that they were related—fraternal or possibly even identical twins—no amount of investigation has ever been able to discover even a distant relationship, and their fingerprints were not at all alike. (This is possibly significant in terms of the theory that they were related. Identical twins, even nonidentical siblings, often have *similar* fingerprints and may even have the same fingerprint classification. But identical fingerprint classifications do not mean that the prints are identical.)

What Are Bertillon Measurements?

French file clerk Alphonse Bertillon invented, in 1879, the first really successful means of criminal identification. Prior to that time, the only means of recognizing a criminal who was trying to get by with an assumed name was by the good memory of police officers. The few descriptions that were made were so vague as to be useless: "tattoo on arm" meant nothing unless a description of what the tattoo looked like and where the tattoo was located on which arm was also provided.

Bertillon's system, called Bertillonage, included a set of fourteen different measurements of different parts of the body, coupled with a *portrait parle*, a very precise system of careful description. Bertillon, however, did an atrocious job of presenting his idea, and when officials finally agreed to let him try it, he was told that if he did not succeed in catching one criminal in the act of changing his name within three months, the entire system would be scrapped.

The chances of having someone arrested, released and then re-arrested under a different name within three months seemed slim; however, Bertillon set to work—and succeeded. Bertillonage at once was the rage worldwide. However, it had several major problems: (1) its success depended on making careful and time-consuming measurements of every person arrested, and at that time very few police were either willing or able to take that time; (2) the *portrait parle* system, although a great improvement over previous systems of description, was too difficult for most people to master; and (3) it was impossible to use Bertillonage on a person who was not already in hand.

Bertillon was extremely bitter as he watched his system go down in defeat before the science of fingerprints. As long as he lived, he fought to keep it alive, at least in France; but immediately on his death, Bertillonage was abandoned even there.

The Roscoe Pitts Case

People have attempted to beat the fingerprint system. In 1941, Robert J. "Roscoe" Pitts was released from Alcatraz, determined to beat the fingerprint system next time. He robbed a warehouse and service station in North Carolina in May, and then headed to New Jersey, where plastic surgeon Leopold Brandenburg agreed to replace the skin of his fingertips with skin grafts from his sides. When the lengthy and painful surgery, which involved having Pitts's hands temporarily grafted to his sides, was finally over, Pitts's fingertips were completely smooth. But in October, when he was arrested in El Paso, Texas, police had no trouble at all identifying him by the prints of his fingers below the tips. Furthermore, a Treasury agent who saw Pitts twenty years later told me that even then Pitts was unable to use his fingertips normally because of their extreme sensitivity to pressure and heat.

With that debacle, petty hoodlum Roscoe Pitts found his way into history. If he hadn't tried to get rid of his fingerprints, nobody would ever have heard of him.

Are Criminals too Smart?

I have heard people—even police officers—say that there has been so much publicity on fingerprints that criminals aren't dumb enough to leave them anymore. Fortunately, that is absolutely untrue. U.S. Department of Justice figures indicate that a constant minimum of one-third of all property crimes result in usable fingerprints, if police would just look for them. The sad fact, however, is that too many police have stopped looking for fingerprints, with the result that too many criminals are getting away with crimes they should not be getting away with.

When my house in Fort Worth was burglarized, it took me several telephone calls to get ident officers to come to the scene. When one finally showed up, she informed me in superior tones that it is impossible to get fingerprints from aluminum screen frames.

That was a lie; aluminum screen frames are one of the best surfaces. But I pretended to assume she was simply ill-informed; I explained my background, borrowed her fingerprint equipment, and lifted several beautiful prints, which I turned over to her. To the best of my knowledge, nothing was ever done with the prints — even when a couple of teenagers who had been burglarizing houses in my neighborhood were arrested.

I visited the Fort Worth ident office and learned why. Despite banks of stored fingerprint cards, they had one person working apparently only part-time on latent comparison, and apparently no attempt at nonsuspect identification was even being made.

Introducing AFIS

In real life, *every* burglary, robbery, recovered stolen auto, theft from auto, sexual assault by an unknown assailant, forgery, and counterfeiting — as well as any other crime in which the use of human hands was involved — should be followed, as soon as possible, by a diligent search for fingerprints. If this were done, and if all legible lifted fingerprints were then checked through AFIS — the Automated Fingerprint Identification System — the conviction rates in some areas would more than triple. In fiction, you may decide whether the department you're writing about does this right, does it in what police would call a half-assed manner, or does it not at all. If you're writing about a real department, find out how good a clearance rate (that is, what percentage of reported crimes are solved) the department has and how much use it makes of fingerprints. Ask politely; people tend to get defensive about these things. In writing about the Fort Worth Police Department, for fairly obvious reasons I tend to avoid mentioning fingerprints. My other series is set in a fictitious town, but it's near the real town of Galveston, and Galveston has a terrific ident section, which I mention fairly often.

Suspect Ident, Nonsuspect Ident

What is the difference between a suspect ident and a nonsuspect ident?

In a suspect ident, a suspect has been developed by other means, and all the identification technician has to do is to compare the latent with one fingerprint card. Anyone who cannot make an ident in that way has no right to call himself or herself an identification technician.

In a nonsuspect ident situation, there is no evidence except the lifted latent. The identification technician must search the latent—that is, compare the latent to a set of fingerprint cards. In Albany, Georgia, we maintained separate sex-crime files and burglar files, so that the print would be searched through the appropriate files (a robber would usually be found in the burglar file, as few people graduate to robbery without first trying burglary). Only in extraordinary cases would we search the entire files; comparing a single print to 10,000 or more fingerprint cards by hand is a monumental task.

Prior to AFIS, even a large police department identification section making as many nonsuspect idents a month as Doc and I were would have had the right to preen. But now, with AFIS, a police department of any size at all that is not making at least twenty to thirty idents a month must be considered lazy or ignorant. One identification officer proudly told me that his department had about a 15 percent ident rate; that is, they made idents on about 15 percent of all latents lifted. That sounded pretty good to me—until I found out his department, in a town eight times the size of Albany, was making fewer latent lifts than Doc and I had been making idents.

How AFIS Works

Let's step back for a moment and talk about fingerprints themselves.

And why do I want to do this? Because a mystery writer can be made to look extremely stupid if s/he misdescribes fingerprints. My dear friend Elizabeth Linington/Lesley Egan/Dell Shannon once severely misdescribed a fingerprint in one of her novels. I gave her a book about fingerprints. In her next novel, she described a "tented whorl." There is no such thing.

Fingerprint Types

There are three main types of fingerprints: *arches*, *loops* and *whorls*. About 35 percent of all fingerprints are whorls; about 5 percent of all fingerprints are arches; and about 60 percent of all fingerprints are loops. These are subdivided into plain arches and tented arches; radial loops and ulnar loops; and plain whorls, double loop whorls, central pocket loop whorls, and accidentals. People often have different patterns on different fingers; whorls are most often found on the thumbs, and arches are most often found on the index and middle finger. Now let's have a look at some of these patterns.

Figure 5-1 illustrates the eight different fingerprint patterns. The drawing of the radial and ulnar loops assumes that the prints are from the right hand; in fact, a radial loop is one in which the direction of flow tends to be in the direction of the thumb, and an ulnar loop is one in which the direction of flow tends to be in the direction of the little finger. Ulnar loops are far more common than radial loops, and radial loops tend most commonly to be found only on the index or index and middle fingers.

There are 1,024 possible primary classifications of fingerprints—and where do we get the primary classification? Figure 5-2 is the rolled print portion of a fingerprint card; remember that below it will be the plain—nonrolled—prints, with all four fingers on each hand printed together, the left hand first, then the left thumb, then the right thumb, then the right four fingers.

The top number in this chart is the finger number. All fingerprint cards use the same finger numbers, so that the prints are always taken in the same order and so that an identification technician will always know, for example, that the number 1 finger is the right thumb and the number 10 finger is the left little finger. Each numbered finger is given a numerical value as shown above, but only the whorls are counted. Arches, tented arches and loops are called "nonnumbered" patterns. The primary classification appears as a fraction, with the sum of the first number in each set of two—that is, fingers number 1, 3, 5, 7 and 9—plus a 1 which is added to each set of numbers, as the denominator and the sum of the second set of numbers—fingers 2, 4, 6, 8 and 10—plus the added 1 as the numerator. For example, suppose that we have whorls on both thumbs and loops everywhere else (this is an extremely common pattern). The primary classification would have a denominator of 16 (from the right thumb, finger #1) plus 1 (the additional 1), or 17, and a numerator of 4 (from the left thumb, finger #6) plus 1 (the additional 1) of 5—hence, 5/17. The single most common primary classification, taking in over half of all fingerprint patterns, is 1/1—that is, there are no whorls at all; therefore, none of the numerical values count except the additional 1 which is always added.

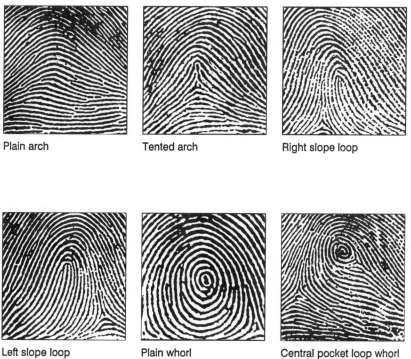

Plain arch   Tented arch   Right slope loop

Left slope loop   Plain whorl   Central pocket loop whorl

Double loop whorl   Accidental whorl

Figure 5-1. The eight fingerprint patterns. Remember that the right slope loop is ulnar on the right hand and radial on the left hand, and the left slope loop is ulnar on the left hand and radial on the right hand.

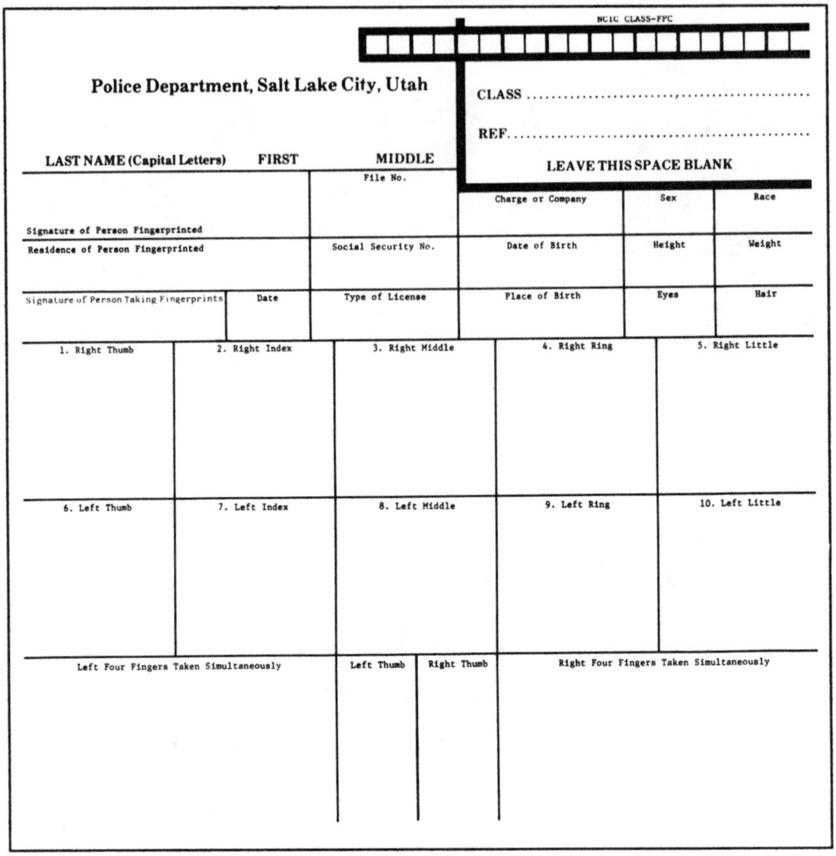

			NCIC CLASS–FPC		

Police Department, Salt Lake City, Utah

CLASS ....,.....................

REF. ....

LAST NAME (Capital Letters) FIRST		MIDDLE	LEAVE THIS SPACE BLANK		
		File No.			
Signature of Person Fingerprinted			Charge or Company	Sex	Race
Residence of Person Fingerprinted		Social Security No.	Date of Birth	Height	Weight
Signature of Person Taking Fingerprints	Date	Type of License	Place of Birth	Eyes	Hair

1. Right Thumb	2. Right Index	3. Right Middle	4. Right Ring	5. Right Little
6. Left Thumb	7. Left Index	8. Left Middle	9. Left Ring	10. Left Little

Left Four Fingers Taken Simultaneously	Left Thumb	Right Thumb	Right Four Fingers Taken Simultaneously

Figure 5-2. A standard fingerprint card. Notice the way the fingers are numbered for the rolled impressions.

You don't have to understand this. You don't even have to try. I have explained it in far greater detail than this to people who then stare at me and exclaim, "That's impossible."

The entire FBI fingerprint classification system—a major refinement of the Henry system—with all its primaries, secondaries, subsecondaries, sub-subsecondaries, finals and so forth, is extremely complicated; even some fingerprint technicians do not understand it fully, and there is no earthly reason to give it here. If you really want to learn it, get a copy of the FBI fingerprint handbook *The Science of Fingerprints*, available from the United States Government Printing Office for about eight dollars; several other very fine fingerprint books are listed in the bibliography.

The NCIC System

The NCIC fingerprint system, although it is based on the Henry system, is not quite the same. We need to get to a little more information before explaining it.

Figure 5-3 shows a loop pattern, with arrows pointing to the *delta* and the *core*. A loop is measured by counting the ridges intervening between the delta and the core.

Figure 5-4 shows a whorl pattern. Whorls theoretically always have at least two deltas (only the very rare *accidental whorl* can have more than two deltas); in fact, as most fingerprint people know, some whorls do not have two deltas. But a whorl is measured by tracing the ridge from the left delta. If it goes more than two ridges inside the right delta, as this one does, it is an *inner trace whorl*. If it meets the right delta within two ridges one way or the other, it is a *meeting trace whorl*. If it goes more than two ridges outside the right delta, it is an *outer trace whorl*. Arches and tented arches are not measured.

For an NCIC classification, a fingerprint would be listed as follows:

A *plain whorl* would be shown as P plus the tracing. Thus, an inner trace plain whorl would be listed as PI.

A *central pocket loop whorl* would be listed as C plus the tracing. Thus a central pocket loop whorl with a meeting trace (which is very uncommon—a central pocket loop is most often an inner or outer trace) would be listed as CM.

A *double loop whorl* would be listed as D plus the tracing. Thus a double loop whorl with an outer trace would be listed as DO.

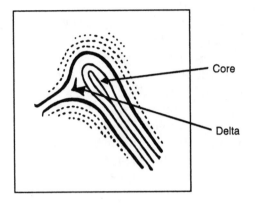

Figure 5-3. Loop pattern. Because two ridges separate the delta and the core, this is a 2-count loop.

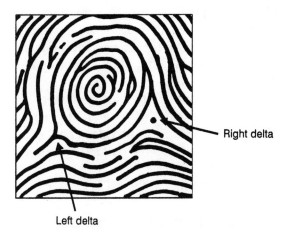

Figure 5-4. Whorl pattern. Ridge tracing begins at left delta and follows around to closest approach to right delta. Because the tracing from the left delta is within two ridges of the right delta, this is a meeting trace.

An *accidental*—which effectively is any print that does not fall into any of the normal classifications—would be listed as X plus the tracing; if there are more than two deltas, the tracing will be from the extreme left delta to the extreme right delta. Thus, an accidental with an outer trace would be listed as XO.

An *ulnar loop* would be listed according to its ridge count: 17, for example, if there are 17 ridges between the delta and the core.

A *radial loop* would be listed according to its ridge count plus 50; thus, a radial loop with 17 ridges between the delta and the core would be listed as 67.

An *arch* is shown as AA and a tented arch as TT.

Ten Arches and Bunny Feet

Remember that arches and tented arches together make up slightly less than 5 percent of all fingerprints; the proportion actually varies very slightly according to race from about 3.5 percent to about 6.5 percent. Arches and tented arches are most commonly found on the index and middle finger. Very few people have arches on all ten fingers; in fact, in Albany, as our total number of fingerprint cards rose from about 10,000 when I first began working with them to around 13,000 by the time I left, the number of all-arch cards remained constant. There were three. Two of them came from people I never met; the third came from Eddie.

Eddie was probably the stupidest burglar I ever met. Knowing from his first trial—assuming, of course, that he paid any attention to it—that he had the rarest ten-finger classification in the world, he went right on burglarizing, and he went right on not wearing gloves.

And Eddie had bunny feet. When law-enforcement people say somebody has bunny feet, they do not mean it as a compliment. A person who has—or grows—bunny feet is a person who has repeatedly escaped from custody.

Eddie burglarized a grocery store, eight doctors' offices, and several other businesses. We caught him. It wasn't too hard; all those arch patterns helped.

Eddie has another strange habit. When he's caught, he denies everything for about two minutes and then he starts to giggle and says, "Well, I guess you got me."

Eddie went to prison.

Eddie grew bunny feet. On his way home, burglarizing in every town he passed through on the way, he stopped and burglarized a sheriff's office in a nearby town.

We caught him. It wasn't too hard; all those arch patterns helped.

Eddie denied everything and then started giggling.

Eddie went to prison again, this time as a habitual offender. A few days later, I met a guard from the prison Eddie had been sent to the second time. I mentioned Eddie and his bunny feet. The guard thanked me for the warning.

I haven't seen Eddie since. But if I ever do, I'll recognize him easily. All those arches help.

Missing or amputated fingers are shown as XX, and patterns so scarred or mutilated that they are unreadable are shown as SR.

Figure 5-5 is a fingerprint card, already classified according to the simple Henry classification, not the FBI extensions. Following is the NCIC classification of that card:

WOTT0305TTDI06TT15TT

That formula would allow any fingerprint technician to reconstruct the classification of the fingerprint card. But it would not allow identification.

Identification by Prints

And here's where we get into what fingerprinting is all about.

If fingerprints were composed entirely of straight or curved complete lines, identification would not be possible. But they are not. These lines stop and start, form islands. The main *minutiae* — identifying points — points of similarity, as identification technicians call them — of fingerprints are ridge endings, dots, short ridges, bifurcations and trifurcations (see Figure 5-6).

It is the arrangement of these identifying points that make identification possible. One of the individual fingerprints I succeeded in memorizing had a long, near-vertical triangle beginning at the delta, which formed the point of one of the angles. Toward the core, it had two long ridges followed by a short ridge. I did not have to memorize the entire print: These few details gave me five

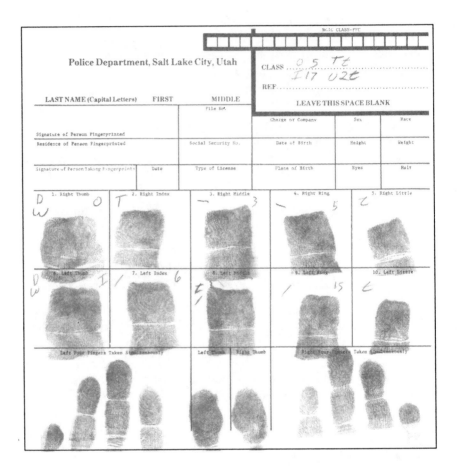

Figure 5-5. A fingerprint card.

Short ridge

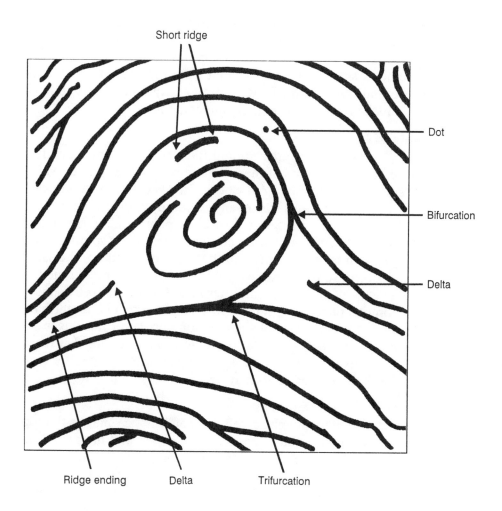

Dot

Bifurcation

Delta

Ridge ending   Delta   Trifurcation

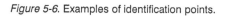

Figure 5-6. Examples of identification points.

points, and as I went through fingerprint cards every day, I could stop and compare any print I found that contained those five points. However, these five points were rare enough that in actual practice I have never seen another fingerprint, out of the hundreds of thousands of individual prints I have looked at, containing these points.

Which brings us to another common question.

Points of Similarity

How many points are required for certainty? Some countries have ruled on this; some of them require twenty-four points, which I consider an idiotic rule. To the best of my knowledge, no jurisdiction in the United States has set any standard. Very few technicians would be satisfied with fewer than eight points unless the points were extremely unusual; I will add that I once saw two prints that had seven points of similarity and that were not made by the same hand. A detective from another police department brought me the prints to look at, and it was only after he left that I realized I should have photographed the prints. I've wished ever since that I had, because that many points of similarity on nonidentical prints is extremely rare. In fact, as odd as this may seem, it is rare that there are any points of similarity on nonidentical prints, no matter how identical their classifications may be.

Determining a Thumbprint

Examine your thumbs carefully. You'll notice that at the top of your right thumb, the ridges tend to flow up and in toward the body. On the left thumb, the ridges at the top tend to flow up and in toward the body as well. This means that when the print happens to include the upper area, it is always possible to tell that it is a thumb, and which hand it belongs on.

The Most-Used Fingers

In burglaries and robberies, the fingers that most often show up are the index and middle fingers of the right hand, with the ring finger and the thumb running a close second and third. Remember, these are fingers 2 and 3 first, 1 and 4 second, according to the fingerprint numbering system. In forgeries, we get fingerprints far less often than we get palm prints—and you'll remember the discussion of palm prints in chapter four.

Among other things, all of this means that any time you have a thumbprint, or any time you have two fingers together, you can always tell which hand was used. If you have just one finger and the print is of a loop, you can be almost certain which hand it is, because radial loops—loops sloping toward the thumb rather than toward the little finger—are rare, and they occur almost solely on the index finger. Therefore, you can make an educated guess as to whether the person who left the print was right-handed or left-handed. With whorls and only one finger, you are on less sure ground; with tented arches, you can rarely make more than a guess; and with plain arches, you'd really have to have at least the smudge of another finger to be sure which hand the print belongs on.

Can Fingerprints Be Forged?

When I first began fingerprint work, we were all assured that fingerprints could not be forged well enough to fool a good identification technician. That may still be true. But what most of us never considered was that a good, but dishonest, identification technician could forge a print and get away with it, as long as no other good identification technician studied his work. And we went on believing that until a case broke that made front pages across the country and was written up in *Reader's Digest*. The answer now is, yes, fingerprints can be forged. And at least one man went to prison on the basis of forged fingerprints.

Here is how the technician did it: First, he photocopied a known fingerprint of the suspect. Next, while the photocopy was still hot, he put fingerprint tape down on it and lifted the print. (This, of course, was perfectly easy to do; remember that powdered photocopier toner is used for fingerprint powder in some situations.) Then he put the tape down on the object he wanted to "find" the print on. And then he photographed the print, with the explanation—perfectly reasonable—that the tape had been put on the print to protect it.

The forgery finally was detected in the following manner: The suspected forgery was compared with all known prints of the one-time suspect, now victim. Although identification points are the same on all prints from the same finger, no two prints themselves should ever be identical, because of slight or great differences in position, pressure, and so forth. Therefore, when an inked print identical in every way to the purported latent was discovered, a strong presumption of forgery was created.

When the story broke in the media—when Doc was out of town and Butch not yet in ident—I knew every person in the police department was going to ask me questions about it. In order to forestall having to answer a hundred-and-eighty-odd different people, as soon as I read the article, I pulled my own fingerprint card out of the applicant file, photocopied it, lifted a print from it, taped it down on a lift card, typed an explanation under it, and put it on the bulletin board. It took me about five minutes, counting typing. That's how easy it was—and if the dishonest technician had destroyed the card he used to create the forgery, he might have gotten away with it.

This means that more than ever, the honor of the technician is on the line when s/he testifies in court.

And this certainly gives you something to play with in fiction.

Now to be fair—Things are possible in small departments, small jurisdictions, that may not be possible in larger ones. When I commented that I had made a nonsuspect ident from a palm print, a task the FBI says is impossible, I will hasten to add that for the FBI it would certainly be impossible. It took me several weeks, and I was working with a universe of fewer than 1,000 palm prints.

In Albany it was practicable—though not very practical—to search a single latent print manually through the entire files as well as through the specialized files, although it might take upwards of a year. In Salt Lake City, with closer to 90,000 fingerprint cards, it would be on the outside edge of practicable, and might take ten years. In New York it would be totally impossible, and the mind boggles at the thought of trying to manually search a single print through the massive FBI files, which at least in theory include every person who's ever been arrested, served in the armed forces, or applied for security clearance in the entire United States. That's why older novels in which a single print is rushed to the FBI without a suspect, and the FBI comes right back and tells who made the print, are totally unrealistic.

Using AFIS

The situation now is quite different. Using its AFIS system, the FBI can make up to one hundred single-print searches through its twenty-three-million-card criminal file in a single night and have the results the next morning. Generally, however, the entire file is not searched; rather, cards fitting within logical parameters are searched. For example, if a bank is robbed in Utah by a perp described as a white male in his mid-forties, the search might begin with a look at all known white male burglars and robbers between thirty-five and fifty-five in Utah, Idaho, Nevada and Colorado. If necessary, the parameters would be repeatedly enlarged until the whole file had been searched.

In the past, even an ambitious and very hard working police department in a very large city found making nonsuspect idents difficult if not impossible, simply because of the quantity of cards that would have to be searched. A department in a town with many transients, no matter what the town's size, would have a terribly difficult time. Only a moderate-sized town with a stable population stood much chance of making the kind of record Doc and I created in Albany, Georgia, and other departments made in such places as Galveston, Texas (despite its large transient population) and Shreveport, Louisiana.

AFIS has changed all that. AFIS, first thought of when computers began to make a large impact on law enforcement in the sixties, was intensively studied in the seventies and first implemented in the late eighties. Although the acronym stands for Automated Fingerprint Identification System, let me say at the outset that the computer itself does not make the identification. The best the computer can do is toss out one or more — up to ten — possibles. The identification itself must be made by the human eye.

Because I left identification work before any AFIS systems were in use, I am indebted for this information to published Department of Justice documents, to Lynn Bergen of the Salt Lake City Police Department crime laboratory, and to the FBI latent fingerprint section.

To start with, there are several different AFIS systems and AFIS networks, and like any other dissimilar computer systems, these cannot "talk" to each other. Furthermore, no state or local police departments are able to tie into the FBI AFIS system, so the dream of being able to search every fingerprint file in the country in minutes or days is still no more than a dream. However, the FBI hopes that by 1995 all police departments will be able to tie into what they call a "latent cognizant data base," which will contain at least a large part, if not all, of the FBI criminal data base.

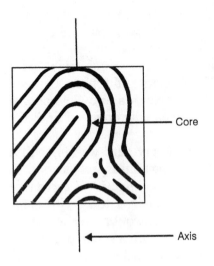

Core

Axis

Figure 5-7. A single print, showing axis of finger.

But from Salt Lake City, it is possible to search more than four million prints inside the state of Utah, and to access the fingerprint files of Alaska, Oregon, Washington, Idaho, Wyoming, Nevada and (with special permission only) California. Call your state crime laboratory to find out what states can be accessed from your jurisdiction, or the nearest real jurisdiction to your imaginary jurisdiction.

And here's how it's done.

Figure 5-7 shows a single fingerprint. The first arrow points to the core of the print. The second arrow points to the axis of the print, which is the midline axis of the finger that made the print. In order to be put on an AFIS system, a latent print must be in a black-on-white format. If the print was processed with black powder and mounted on a white card, it is already in the correct format. If it is in any other format, the following steps must be taken:

First, the technician photographs the latent. The photograph is then enlarged five times, and the technician carefully traces the latent in black ink on white tracing paper. The tracing is then photographed and reduced back down to a one-to-one size, and the result is taken to the computer.

The unknown latent, or the reproduction of the tracing, is placed in the computer, and the technician manually sets cross hair references, similar to the cross hairs on an aiming device, on the core and the axis. The computer then rotates the print to approximately 15 degrees left and right of the axis, plotting where minutiae — those points of identification we've already talked about — fall. The larger the number of points, the larger the numerical rating the computer assigns the latent, and the larger the numerical rating, the higher are the chances of an identification — although a few AFIS hits have been made with as few as eight points.

In addition, the computer may be given specific parameters, such as whether this print is from a male, a female, or sex unknown; what race it is or race unknown; a specific or approximate birthdate or birthdate unknown; and so forth.

Distinguishing Sex and Race From Fingerprints

It's impossible. Although there are very slight statistical differences in race, the differences are nowhere near enough to determine what race a person is. There is no discernable difference whatever in sex; although size is sometimes an indicator, a large woman will leave larger prints than a small man. A witness might help, but remember what I said about eyewitness testimony . . . and thereby hangs a tale.

A woman was attacked and raped in her bedroom. Although all her lights were out, there was good light coming in from a street light just outside her bedroom window. The MO fit a known rapist in her neighborhood, but he was black, and she said the man who attacked her was a white man with a bushy beard.

Detective Larry Grey picked up an extremely good latent from her window glass, a thumb print outside and a smudged index fingerprint inside, so although the index fingerprint was unreadable, we were sure the prints had been made after the glass was removed from the window. I searched the print through known white sex criminals and known white burglar files. Finding no match, I filed the print.

Several months later, when things were quiet, I was re-searching old latents. When I came to that one, I felt a little lazy. It happened that because the number of sex criminals in Albany was fairly small, we had black and white filed together, and I knew I had a right thumbprint. The right thumb is always in the same place on every fingerprint card, but because of changes in the design of fingerprint cards, race can be noted in any of several places. I decided it was easier just to check the print than to check the race.

I made a very quick ident. She was attacked by the man Larry and I had thought of from the first — and she was so panicked that she could not remember, by the time Larry talked with her, what race her assailant had been. Her white man with a bushy beard was in fact a black man with a bushy beard.

I do not like eyewitness testimony.

The computer then begins to search for similar prints in its data base. It produces up to ten candidates and then displays the candidate prints beside the latent on a dual screen, so that the identification technician can make the preliminary comparisons. If the prints seem close enough, the technician then, still with the computer, goes into the data base and pulls out an image of the card itself, to make a definitive comparison. Eventually, if the identification seems positive, the technician will compare the fingerprint card itself with the latent.

It is important to remember that no identifications are made by, or even from, the computer itself. A computer is not capable of making fingerprint identifications; rather, the computer reads what are called *events*—that is, breaks in ongoing patterns.

And what have the results been?

Most fingerprint technicians—including me—on first hearing of the plans for AFIS, back in the seventies, felt extremely dubious. We felt, correctly, that it would be impossible for a computer to take into account and allow for all the distortions, changes and so forth that result from position and pressure, that the human eye adjusts for so easily.

Every technician who has ever worked with AFIS has been wild about it. It does not, as we assumed correctly from the start, replace the trained eye of the skilled fingerprint examiner. What it does do is eliminate about 95 percent of the scut work, the time-consuming work, and allow the examiner to accomplish far more in less time. A latent can be searched through 50,000 cards in less than an hour; the technician then has to actually compare only about ten individual prints. The total expenditure of time, not counting getting the latent and doing the charting to take it into court, might be no more than two hours. Searching manually, squeezing the work in among all the other work an identification bureau is constantly doing, it might take five years to search a single latent through 50,000 cards.

Fingerprint cards, involving all ten fingers, also may be searched through AFIS. According to the Department of Justice, in a pilot study on AFIS, which is listed in the bibliography, "Search time for a ten-print search (rolled print to rolled print comparison) in a file of under 500,000 is a matter of minutes" (5). This is extremely important, because criminals like to give false names. In the past, although a fingerprint card on every arrestee was routinely sent to the FBI, it might take several weeks for the card to be classified and manually searched, and in that time a badly wanted person, picked up for a minor offense, might be back on the street and gone. And it's frustrating to find out that cop-killer you picked up for public intox, and released after he served his three days, has vanished again. That no longer happens in a jurisdiction that uses AFIS.

The Department of Justice pilot study says that in the first two years of development, the California Identification System "entered

420,000 fingerprint cards into the file that is used for latent searching. The file includes persons born in 1950 or later who have been convicted of a felony, a group that is estimated to represent only 34 percent of the AFIS data base but 47 percent of daily AFIS activity. . . . In its first year of operation, the San Francisco Police Department's AFIS system conducted 5,514 latent print searches and made 1,001 identifications. . . . [They] cleared 816 of those cases, including 52 homicides, compared to 58 cases cleared the previous year on the basis of latent print identifications" (13). That set of statistics alone says all that needs to be said on the value of AFIS.

Bear in mind that all of these are nonsuspect identifications, what the Department of Justice refers to as "cold makes." Generally one hit on a nonsuspect search will clear from one to twenty or more crimes, because criminal MO's are fairly recognizable, and because a search warrant, issued on the basis of such a hit, is likely to find the proceeds of several crimes.

You may, legitimately, wonder whether the attention of ident people ever wavers. Do matches slip by? How often?

I can't answer that, of course. I have never known a match to slip by, but if it slipped by me, of course I wouldn't know. Probably matches do slip by. That's not ideal, of course. But I do know that no legitimate identification person ever, under any circumstances, goes to court and claims a match when there is not one.

That's what's most important, when you're talking about someone's liberty, perhaps someone's life.

What does this mean in fiction? It means what you want to make it mean. You can let your criminal leave his print and be caught by AFIS. You can let your criminal be too smart to leave his prints, or you can let his prints be so pressure-distorted that AFIS can't read them. You decide — but the technology is there, and as a citizen, you certainly have the right to demand that your jurisdiction use it, no matter what you do in fiction.

TABLE 5

How You Can Use Experts

A theory says that *provided you do your library research first* you should be able to locate any known fact (as long as it is neither a government secret nor a proprietorial trade secret), in a maximum of five telephone calls.

When I heard that, I couldn't believe it. So I tested it—and it worked! I then began passing the theory on to my students, and they also tested it. It worked for them, too, and it will work for you.

But you have to do it right. Here's how:

1. Use the best library accessible to you, and look up all you can find (within reason) about whatever the question is.
2. From your reading, or from common sense, determine who is likely to be the most convenient expert on that topic. Be cautious! Some people claim expertise in subjects they are not in fact experts in. (I am a fingerprint expert. I am not a firearms expert. I asked many questions about firearms in the course of writing this book.)
3. Formulate a list of intelligent questions.
4. Telephone the expert.
5. Introduce yourself and ask whether this is a convenient time to talk.
6. If it is not, ask when you may call back.
7. When you reach your expert with time to talk, ask your questions.
8. Don't stick so rigidly to those questions that you don't follow a lead the expert gives you that opens up something you hadn't thought of. But don't ramble all over the universe; experts are busy people.
9. Thank your expert, and ask permission to call again if you come to a point you don't understand.

Of course it works—and almost always, your expert will not only be delighted to tell you but will even look up information for you. As I write this, I am extremely grateful to Utah gunsmith Mark McComb for spending hours looking up names of modern manufacturers of single-shot revolvers, after I read a book that said nobody manufactures single-shot revolvers anymore. (And this is an example of being careful about our experts. The guy who wrote the book was fairly up on firearms. But Mark makes them, repairs them, sells them, and loves them. He was the real expert.)

Why are these experts so happy to talk to you? Look at it this way: You become an expert only on something that interests you. If it interests you, you not only want to learn about it, you also want to talk about it. So you talk about it, and talk about it, and talk about it, until all those around you are sick of hearing about it.

And now what happens? Some fresh new person calls and actually *wants* you to talk about your pet topic! It's terrific!

How would you feel, if you were the expert?

That's how they feel. Not one in a thousand will grouch at you or want to charge you for the advice — and if you do get a grouch, that's all right. Start looking for another expert.

IDENTIFYING HUMAN REMAINS

It often happens that a corpse cannot be identified on account of decomposition being too far advanced and neither the structure of the body nor the articles of clothing, etc., found on the deceased showing any peculiarity to aid identification. And yet the identification may . . . be of the greatest importance.

— Hans Gross,
Criminal Investigation

Now, as in 1934, identification of a corpse may present extreme difficulty. In one case I worked, a transient who had been in the habit of sleeping in a storeroom where volatile oils were stored accidentally set the oils afire. The body was burned beyond recognition; the only thing I could tell for certain was that the victim's left and right ears were distinctly different in size and the smaller ear was set somewhat higher on the head than the larger. The transient, whose name we knew, seemed the most likely person to have burned to death in the fire. I went to talk with the transient's brother and eventually, reluctantly, took the brother to view the remains.

The brother was adamant that his brother had not had any difference in the size of his ears, and therefore this could not be his brother.

I spent the better part of the next week checking out all possible leads as to who else could have been sleeping there and where the missing man was if he was not in fact in the morgue. But every lead brought me back to the same place. Arrest photos of the transient were useless, as they showed his full face and one profile but not the other, and the full face was not adequate to determine differences in ears.

I kept looking, and finally found one photograph in which a new technician had taken the wrong profile for a mug shot — so finally I had two photographs, one of the left side of the head and one of the right, to lay side by side. I took them back to the brother, showing him irrefutable evidence that his brother's ears were indeed somewhat mismatched.

Staring at the photos, he said, "I'll be damned! You know, I never had noticed that before."

And at last, our corpse had a name.

The Condition of the Remains

That one was hard enough. But what about cases in which all identification points — handprints, footprints, ears, facial features — have been completely removed, either deliberately to prevent identification, or simply as a result of advanced decomposition?

Many corpses, many skeletons, are never identified. But science continues to close in on even the most difficult cases.

At this point, I want to warn readers that some of the contents of this chapter will be offensive to those with weak stomachs. When you are writing fiction, you can decide how graphic or how vague you want to be. But I have the responsibility to tell you what really happens, what things really look like and smell like. If you're not sure of the stability of your stomach, do not eat while reading.

Beyond Identification

Bear in mind, also, that what I have said in this book about determining the cause of death is no more than scratching the surface. For a far more definitive study aimed at writers rather than at pathologists, I recommend Keith Wilson's *Cause of Death*, Writer's Digest Books, 1992.

Identification is not the only thing that must be done about a corpse, and in many cases identification falls rather late in the process. So let's start from the beginning. We have a corpse. Or we have a skeleton. Or we have bone fragments that might eventually, if we're lucky, add up to a skeleton. What do we do? In what order?

Where to Start?

Always—always—always—the first thing we do is take photographs and measurements—that triangulation we spoke of in chapter one. Note the body position: Is it face up? Face down? Hands drawn in toward the body? Hands extended, or stretched out above the body? In the case of a fire, very often the arms are bent at the elbows, hands clenched into fists, as if the person were in a defensive position in a boxing match. This, called the *pugilist position*, frequently is assumed by the unknowledgeable to mean the person was trying to fight an assailant; in fact, it has to do with the contraction of muscles as a result of the heat, and has no further meaning.

Cadaveric Spasm

In the case of violent death not involving a fire, here are some things to look for: Is anything in the hands? In the case of *absolutely instantaneous* death when the muscles were in work at the time of death, the body may go into an instant cadaveric spasm, which precedes, and may be mistaken for, ordinary rigor mortis; indeed, some pathologists maintain that it is an unusual instant rigor mortis. In this case, whatever the person was holding at the time of death is clutched permanently—and if you're lucky, that might be part of the hair or clothing of the assailant.

A Suicide That Was: Cadaveric Spasm

I was called about midnight. Her husband, a petty gangster, was in a rage, fighting like a wild thing; he didn't want any pictures taken, and it took several strong male officers to hold him as I went by with my camera to enter their beautiful, very expensive house. She was in a locked bedroom, and again, it took several of us to break the door down and find her lying on her bed, the pistol still pressed to her head. She was in a cadaveric spasm; it took three of us to pry her hand open to remove the pistol.

She'd been making chocolate chip cookies earlier in the day, before she and her husband began quarreling. Some of the cookies had been set out on the table to cool, and others were still stuck to the pan, where she had left them when the shouting began. Her son, who had left the house when the quarreling started and returned when he saw police cars converging, was in the living room crying, and I tried to talk with him to no avail.

It wasn't until years later, when he and his aunt were living in the same apartment complex I was and his father was in prison on a totally unrelated charge, that I learned the boy sincerely believed that his father had murdered his mother and the police just hadn't figured that out. I explained to the aunt, and asked her to explain to the boy, that the position of the pistol, and the cadaveric spasm, made it absolutely impossible for anybody but the victim herself to have fired the fatal shot.

I don't know whether it helped him or not. But he had only one parent left alive, and no matter what his father had in fact done, there was no reason to let him go through life believing his father guilty of that one crucial crime he *hadn't* committed.

Unusual Coloration of the Body

You already know to look for the color and type of the clothing, but what about any unusual coloration of the skin? Most people are aware that carbon monoxide poisoning will turn the skin on a white person a bright cherry red; although this coloration might be less visible on a person with darker skin, it can still be noted in areas that are normally light in color, such as the palms of the hands, the soles of the feet, various mucus membrane surfaces in the mouth and other places. Other conditions might cause other unusual colorations. Note this as carefully as you can in your notes, and don't count on a photograph to show it: Very few color films are able to show such subtle gradations in color.

Defense Wounds and Hesitation Wounds

Are there defense wounds? In a knife murder, almost always the hands, particularly the area between the wrist and the little finger, will have multiple cuts, usually parallel, stretching from the little finger to the wrist and sometimes above the wrist, caused by the victim's attempts to ward off the knife. Sometimes a gunshot victim at close range will show one or more defense wounds if s/he attempted to grab the muzzle of the gun at the time it was firing.

Is there a question whether it is suicide or murder? If it involves slashed wrists or throat, check for hesitation cuts. Very few people will commit suicide with one slash; there are almost always several small hesitation cuts while the person was working on his or her nerve. A lack of hesitation wounds is likely — though certainly not definite — evidence of murder.

Other Visible Marks

What other visible wounds and marks are there? If there are no more than one or two wounds, photographs and measurements may be adequate by themselves. But I have seen victims of multiple stab wounds in which it was necessary, after the body was adequately cleaned, to lay a piece of tracing paper over the body and mark the location of each wound.

If it is a stabbing and you have a suspect weapon, never attempt to fit the knife into the wound. Let the medical examiner (or whoever does the postmortem examination) decide whether this knife could have made this wound. Bear in mind that if the wound looks very slightly smaller than the weapon, that does not always rule out the weapon; the skin stretches. (This applies to gunshots also. A .38-caliber bullet does not always leave what looks like a .38-caliber entry wound. The exit wound is another matter; it may look like a .45 or a shotgun, depending on what happened to the bullet inside the body.)

Was the shooting at close range? If so, there will be powder tattooing, and possibly even visible grains of powder or burns from the muzzle flash, on the skin and/or the clothing.

Spontaneous Human Combustion

And what about spontaneous human combustion — that is, cases reported in *Fate* magazine and various Fortean books and tabloids in which a living person suddenly, without warning, bursts into flame? Scientists say that it does not occur; other people insist they have witnessed it, and scientists do not seem to be able to adequately explain away situations in which the body is burnt to ashes but nothing else in the room, except perhaps the chair or bed on which the remains are lying, is even singed. Even less can they explain cases in which the remains are on a street or sidewalk and witnesses insist they saw the person burst into flames.

I never saw a case of spontaneous human combustion. But many people with no apparent reason to lie insist they have seen it. And I can't help remembering that for many hundreds of years scientists insisted stones could not fall from the sky, while common people went right on seeing meteors turn into meteorites.

I doubt I'll ever want to use spontaneous human combustion in my fiction; I couldn't get away with it. But on the other hand, I couldn't get away with having my villain eaten by the Loch Ness Monster's cousin, although it was a perfect denouement when Gladys Mitchell did it. So if you want to use spontaneous human combustion, be my guest. I'm not going to say it doesn't happen. Just be sure you're writing a book in which you can get away with that kinky an idea.

Postmortem Lividity

Postmortem lividity confuses people who have never before seen a corpse except at a funeral, after it has been cleaned up. Briefly, this is what it means.

At the time of death, the blood, which has been flowing, ceases to flow. Slowly, it pools in the lowermost parts of the body, causing them gradually to assume a deep purplish-red color (or, in the case of carbon monoxide poisoning, a cherry-red color). However, portions of the lowermost part of the body that are under great pressure may at the same time bleach out, so that white creases are visible in the midst of the purplish-red color. A novice, seeing these marks, is likely to assume they are the result of severe bruising. But they are not; they are entirely normal. (And my thanks here go to Detective Billy Johnson, who explained this to me in great detail the first time I saw it.)

This lividity may begin to appear as early as twenty minutes after death or as late as four hours; it is usually complete within about twelve hours. Thus, it is a rather poor indicator of time of death. But it has other uses.

If, when the body is found, the postmortem lividity is consistent with the present body position, it means nothing, except that its degree should be noted, as it may help later a little bit in determining how long the body has been dead. But there is another little peculiarity: postmortem lividity occurs and then does not change. This means that if the body has been in one position for several hours, and then is moved, the lividity will indicate the original position, not the new one. This may be of great help in determining where and in what position the body originally fell or was placed.

Rigor Mortis

And what about rigor mortis — the extreme stiffness which follows death, such that it may take several strong people to change the position of the body? It is *not* true that the medical examiner — or the experienced officer — can glance at the body, assess the extent of rigor mortis, and determine at once how long the body has been dead. You've already heard of cadaveric spasm, which seems to be — or perhaps is — instant rigor mortis. But other things affect timing. I've seen the body of a previously vigorous and healthy man who'd scarcely begun rigor mortis after eighteen hours; I've seen total rigor mortis in the body of an emaciated crib-death baby who'd definitely been alive two hours before I saw her.

Normally rigor mortis begins within two to six hours and is complete within another two to six hours. "Rigidity . . . begins to develop in the muscles of the face, jaw, upper extremities, trunk and lower extremities, appearing in about the sequence mentioned . . ." (Gonzales 56). Prior to rigor mortis, some muscles relax; typically the jaw drops open. However, the eyes normally remain open. (Among other things, this means that the only time an expression on the face of the corpse would be readable — if then — would be in the case of cadaveric spasm, as the muscular relaxation that characteristically precedes rigor mortis would smooth out even the most horrified of expressions. Why do I mention this? Reread *The Hound of the Baskervilles* for the horrified expression on the corpse of the last of the Baskervilles. Yes, I did it, too, in *Too Sane a Murder*, and you are welcome to continue to describe the expression on the corpse. Just be aware it wouldn't really be there.)

Rigor mortis normally lasts, after becoming complete, for about twenty-four to forty-eight hours, leaving in the same order in which it began. In general, rigor mortis in a physically strong person will begin faster and last longer than rigor mortis in a weak or emaciated person, which begins later and lasts a much shorter time. In a hot location as opposed to one with a moderate temperature, rigor mortis begins faster and ends faster; in a very cold location, rigor mortis begins faster but ends far more slowly, and at times it may be impossible to distinguish between rigor mortis and frozen remains.

Body Temperature

Body temperature may not be a very good indicator of time of death. Even under normal conditions, loss of body heat is not a constant, but rather a function of such things as the body temperature at the time of death, the ambient air temperature, and the weight of the body and the person's normal health before death. It may be greatly affected by lying in the sun, lying in a cold room, or by the cause of death; in fact, in the case of violent, painful death—especially prolonged painful death—the core body temperature may continue to rise for up to an hour after death.

In an unattended death in which the body is found intact and fairly promptly, if the first technician who arrives puts an anal thermometer in the body and puts a room thermometer in the room, checking both after half an hour, some indication of time of death may be derived—except that if the death is at all suspicious, the use of the anal thermometer would disturb the crime scene, causing more problems than a possible body temperature might solve. An oral thermometer in this situation is quite useless, as the mouth temperature after death does not reflect the core body temperature, whereas an anal temperature at least might. I've been told that in some jurisdictions, the medical examiner's investigators will make a small puncture in the abdomen and insert the thermometer there. Although that would certainly provide a correct core body temperature, it seems to me that it could also confuse later investigation. I would not do it myself. But you decide what your investigators do— or check with your coroner's office or medical examiner's office to find out what is really done in your jurisdiction.

Motion May Continue

In some situations, it seems that the nerves remain responsive to the last message sent by the brain long after the person is actually dead. Gonzales tells of a man whose myocardium (part of the heart muscle) continued to beat, although the rest of the heart did not, when the body was actually well into rigor mortis. I personally saw a man whose lungs continued to work for half an hour after his brain was blasted out of his skull by a shotgun. Very early in this century,

a few sadistic officers in the army of the Shah of Iran would, for their own amusement, bet on how far a standing con- demned man could run after having been beheaded by sword. One by one the victims had their heads lopped off as they started to run. Some of them ran for considerable distances.

(Kevorkian 57)

Your guess is as good as mine on what "considerable distances" means in this context.

Bodily Processes After Death

But eventually—normally in seconds, sometimes in minutes or more, the body becomes still. The blood clots and then, in some cases, reliquifies, to the extent that at various times of major crisis both the Soviet and the German armies were practicing blood transfusion from cadavers. Postmortem lividity begins; rigor mortis begins. Gradually, over the next few hours, days and weeks, the body begins to succumb to bacteria. The body tissues and blood vessels, as well as body cavities, begin to fill with gas, which causes the entire body to distend. Decay may cause the body to turn any or all of red, green, brown and black. (Folklore says that a white person will tend to turn black in decay and a black person will tend to turn white in decay. I have never seen anything—either in cases I worked or in reference books I have read—to support such a legend, and I do not believe it.) The eyes appear to bulge, the tongue begins to protrude through the swollen lips, and the penis may appear to be erect.

> Blood may begin to be pushed out of the nose, stomach contents from the mouth and fecal material from the anus. This pressure may cause a postmortem expulsion of the fetus from the pregnant uterus. . . . The gas formation in the blood vessels may force fluid, air or liquid fat between the epidermis and the dermis [the upper and lower skin layers] to produce a large blister which may rupture. The skin epithelium and the hair and nails may be easily separated from the dermis by disintegration at the roots. When the nutrient material is used up, the formation of gas ceases and the swelling gradually subsides; the gas leaves the tissues, usually by escaping as a result of damage to the structure or by drainage through a postmortem wound.

(Gonzales 63)

It is important to know these signs of decomposition, because some of them can easily be mistaken for the signs of a death by strangulation, in which the eyes bulge, the tongue protrudes through swollen lips, the penis is typically erect, and the nose may bleed. However, in strangulation the neck may be compressed, the hyoid bone and the thyroid and cricoid cartilages are normally crushed. During a postmortem examination, neck bruises may be visible on the dermis (the inner layer of skin) even if they were not visible on the epidermis (the outer layer of skin).

Of course, heat and humidity tend to speed the process of decomposition, whereas cold and dryness tend to retard it — almost permanently, if extreme cold or dryness continues.

The Ice Man and the Bog Man

Climbers in Switzerland in late summer of 1991 spotted the body of another climber, lodged inside a crack in a glacier. They went back down the mountain and notified officials, and soon the mountain was swarming with rescue workers — who were about four thousand years too late.

Sometime around the year 2800 B.C.E., the man set off across the ice, wearing boots stuffed with straw, trousers, and a lined jacket, carrying all he was likely to need, including a stone knife. Somehow, he slipped and fell into a crevasse. When he was found, his body appeared to have been freeze-dried. Even his eye color was preserved; with his intact clothing and intact tool kit, he was, exultant scientists proclaimed, probably the greatest treasure-trove of neolithic knowledge ever found, and the two countries across whose boundary the glacier lay at once began arguing about which he belonged to.

Crime scene? Probably not — and yet, what was he doing crossing that glacier alone? Did he have companions? Did they try to get help? Did they realize he was dead and reluctantly leave him? Or — did they push him in and keep going?

When peatcutters found a body in a bog in Denmark, they knew they had a murder; the dark-haired man — probably in his mid-forties — still wore around his neck the willow wand with which he had been strangled. But law-enforcement officials were about two thousand years too late for either him or the fourteen-year-old blond girl buried a few feet away from him.

Investigation — archaeological, not criminal — finally suggested he had been strangled as a sacrifice to the goddess Nertha; the girl—judging from the way her hair had been cut away from one side of her head—might have been executed for adultery. But—why were the two bodies so close together? Had she committed adultery with the intended sacrifice, the intended husband of Nertha?

There's no knowing, now. What is known is that some substances—oak water, bog water, and oddly enough, arsenic—preserve a body about as well as, and sometimes better than, freezing does. (In fact, for many years arsenic was a common component of embalming fluid. Imagine trying to prove arsenic poisoning after exhuming one of *those* bodies!)

Moral: Don't commit your murders with arsenic, and watch where you conceal the body, if you want the body to decay quickly.

Bodies Under Water

Humidity is one thing; water is another. Bodies under water begin to decay in an extremely odd way. The fatty tissues of the body begin to react with the water to develop a waxy substance, yellowish-white in color, called *adipocere*, a form of insoluble soap. Gonzales says adipocere "has a rancid odor, floats in water, and dissolves in ether and alcohol." Adipocere eventually replaces the muscles and viscera, as well as the fatty tissues around the face; as it is very light, it is larger in bulk than the tissues it replaces, and the body, especially the face, may take on an extremely grotesque, irregular, bloated appearance.

Adipocere formation may become

> complete in adult bodies in from a year to a year and a half, and in full-term newborn infants in from about six to seven weeks; it does not occur in a fetus of less than seven months' gestation because the composition of the fat at this stage is not suitable for its development.

> (Gonzales 68)

When a body in which much of the tissues have been replaced with adipocere is removed from the water, it is extremely light in weight. The stench is beyond words, far worse than the normal smell of a decaying body (which is bad enough—and as unforgettable as it is indescribable); and the appearance is even more jarring. The mind refuses to accept the fact that what was once a human being can now look like that; it *must* be something made up by set dressers for a horror movie.

Bodies in Dry Climates

On the other hand, bodies in an extremely dry climate may mummify—that is, the fluids evaporate without the tissues rotting—and still be in fairly good condition centuries later. However, even an extremely well mummified body may resume decomposition after hundreds, even thousands, of years if the surrounding atmospheric conditions change.

The Exceptions

And there are always exceptions, partial exceptions. A body in hot, dry air may mummify in places and decompose in other places, particularly where body parts are pressed together or are in a tight location from which fluids cannot easily evaporate. I once saw the body of a man who had committed suicide by asphyxiating himself in his automobile, which he had hidden in the woods. The body was found eight days after the man went missing, and I can still remember word for word the telephone call that told me. Barbara Brackman was dispatching. When I answered the phone, she said, "I'm afraid we've found Oscar" (not his real name).

This was only a few days after the Jackson Street Corpse, and Oscar went missing before the Jackson Street corpse was killed. I had a pretty good idea what I was on my way to, and I said, "Shit! Dead?"

Barbara assured me that he was dead. When I arrived at the scene about twenty minutes later I had to agree: he was definitely, indisputably dead.

I've already told you a little about this one, about the Georgia Bureau of Investigation agents arguing about which one of them was *not* going to open the door and photograph the corpse. In general, the body was fairly well preserved, given how long it had been and how hot and humid the weather was. One of the windows was a couple of inches open, and that had been enough to allow some of the fluids to evaporate. But the head, which was inside a plastic bag that had allowed no evaporation, was almost totally reduced to a skull. The body was stretched across the front seat of a car with the feet jammed against the door on the driver's side and the right hand thrust down between the seat and the wall on the passenger's side. The position of the right arm, like that of the head, had not allowed evaporation, and when we finally opened the passenger's door (we — actually I — had begun with the driver's door, so as to get some photos before the body was moved at all), the right arm fell off.

I've already given you a partial description of the Jackson Street Corpse. After eight days partially wrapped in a wet quilt, in a humid late August in which it had rained several days, decomposition was far advanced, and the smell extended for about a block in any direction. But those weren't the things that bothered me. The Jackson Street Corpse was the only one that ever gave me nightmares, and here's why: Flies had laid eggs in the corpse. Those eggs had hatched, gone quickly through the larva (maggot) stage, metamorphosed into flies, and laid more eggs. When I first saw the body, there seemed to be millions of maggots, seething white footballs of constant motion. I dreamed about those maggots off and on for weeks, until — almost six months later — in my final dream, the maggots turned into baby squirrels, climbed a tree, and ran off, and I never dreamed about them again.

The crime scene at which I came closest to actually throwing up didn't even include a corpse. The corpse had been removed several days earlier, and Doc and I had to go back over there to check out some things that had come up. The only parts of the corpse remaining were part of one earlobe and the smell — along with the smell of rotten onions, rotten cabbage, rotten potatoes and kerosene. When we got away from the scene I told Doc, who was driving, that he had to stop at the next convenience store so that I could get a Coke; otherwise I was going to be sick.

He informed me that I was not allowed to be sick. He had made that quite clear exactly four days after I was sworn in, when I found myself sticking my camera into a skull from which the brain had been removed during autopsy, photographing the .22 slugs where they had lodged behind the eyeballs when the man had been shot in the back of the head.

That had been three years earlier, and I had never gotten sick at a crime scene (and in fact never did). But that day I told Doc that if he did not stop and let me get a Coke he was going to find out very quickly whether or not I was allowed to get sick.

I got the Coke.

I hope you're not trying to eat your supper as you read this.

The Blue Springs Plantation Corpse

One more story, and then I'll leave this part of the subject. Three men were once riding in a car. One of them was holding a shotgun. The shotgun went off when the car hit a bump, and one of the men, struck full in the face, was instantly killed. The other two men, panicking utterly, took the body out in the country onto a pecan plantation and dumped it. The weather was fairly cool for the South, and when the body was found a short time later, most of it was perfectly preserved. Fingerprinting the corpse took no more than about half an hour, and the prints were so good that I was able to identify the corpse from the prints in only about five minutes. But the wounds had looked appetizing to small rodents—opossums and so forth—and the entire skin and tissue of the face, including the eyes, down to but not below the skull, had been totally consumed. When I first saw the corpse, I saw a man lying on his back, fully clothed, arms outstretched, legs slightly spread apart. He could have been only sleeping, except that he had a skull for a face.

Identifying the Remains

That story moves us into the second main topic for this chapter, identifying the remains. That corpse was easily identifiable; his fingertips were in excellent condition, and his prints were on file. The U.S. military services have begun to store a small amount of genetic material from each service person, so that a body—no matter how damaged—can be identified by genetic "fingerprinting" (which we'll discuss in chapter seven). In the future, there will be no more "unknown soldiers." But again, this is working with material deliberately stored for the purposes of identification.

What if there are no fingerprints stored? What if there is no genetic material stored?

Sometimes—if there is an idea as to the corpse's identity— objects belonging to that person may be fingerprinted for comparison with an unknown corpse. The FBI disaster squad, which has the responsibility for identifying all corpses from civilian airplane crashes in the United States, once identified the body of an unknown woman from fingerprints on the hairbrush of the woman they thought she might be.

But even stored fingerprints do no good if no fingerprints can be obtained from the corpse. What do you do then?

Very often, when the epidermis is nearly or totally destroyed, the dermis skin is still more or less intact, and it has the same fingerprint pattern as the epidermis layer except that the ridges are very fragile . . . and finally, as I've been promising, we're back to the Jackson Street Corpse, which began in chapter one.

Back to the Jackson Street Corpse

I did a complete crime scene, which took about ten work-hours on several successive days. We discovered that at some point prior to being moved to the bamboo thicket, the body had been laid between the mattress and the box springs. Meanwhile, detectives talking with uniform officers found that on the last day the shotgun house was known to be occupied, there had been three calls from neighbors reporting yelling and fighting. On the first two calls, police had talked to all three winos, each time telling them they had to keep the noise down. The third time, only two had been present. They had been distinctly nervous, and had promised there would be no more noise. That time, we all surmised, uniform officers had been called before the third man died and arrived after he died. Unfortunately, the uniform men could not remember which two of the three they had seen the third time.

Meanwhile, the medical examiner, wearing a gas mask to do his autopsy, discovered the victim had died of a crushing blow to the back of his head. The crime lab, working with the evidence I had taken there (which had included virtually every portable item which could by the wildest stretch of the imagination have been involved in the crime), discovered evidence that someone had fallen backwards and landed on his head on a small portable space heater.

At the worst, it was manslaughter; more likely, it was accidental death. But two drunks, with a corpse in the house and cops at the door, had panicked. Most likely, this is what happened: When they realized police were on their way again, they hastily stuffed the body between the mattress and the box springs and possibly — probably — at least one of them then lay down on the bed. After the uniform officers left, the surviving two winos got their companion back out of the bed and bent the body double at the waist, covered him with a quilt, fastened his head and feet together with wire coat hangers, took him into the bamboo thicket in the backyard, and left him there, with a couple of sheets of plyboard laid over him. Both then hit the road—and went on drinking. I never saw the third wino, but I did talk to the second, many months later. He'd totally blanked out the whole thing. When I told him what had happened in the house that night, he watched me intently as I spoke and then said, "Lady, if that's what you say, then I guess that's what happened. But I'm damned if I remember a second of it."

And he wasn't lying.

What did we do about it?

Nothing. What good would it have done? We'd never be able to prove which of the two killed the victim, and more than likely nobody had deliberately harmed anyone. The most we could have gotten anybody on was improper disposal of a human body. And again—what good would it have done?

But I'm getting ahead of myself. After doing the crime scene, we—the detectives (mainly Bob Morris) and I—returned to the problem of identifying the body. We had three possibles. The man was wearing a belt buckle with a name on it, but we knew these men wore each other's clothes. The mother of the man who owned the belt buckle viewed the only piece of intact body—a few inches of the back of the neck where the skin had not disintegrated—and insisted that was her son. The coroner said we could not accept that identification; too many people have backs of the neck that look alike.

In the end, the following morning, after I had all other evidence that was going to the crime lab loaded into the car, the coroner and I went to the morgue where the body was floating in a lead tank of formaldehyde. The coroner neatly snipped off both hands at the wrists, dropped them into plastic buckets of formaldehyde, and directed me to take them to the crime laboratory in Atlanta.

So off I drove to Atlanta, with two decaying hands crawling with maggots floating in open buckets of formaldehyde in the front passenger's floorboard of the car, and every Boris Karloff movie I'd ever seen or heard of dancing through my brain. It took me about four hours to drive from Albany to Atlanta and to get all the evidence unloaded and turned over to the scientists at the lab.

And then I headed for home, light of heart and heavy of foot because that ghastly stuff was now out of my car, which wasn't exactly my car because the one Doc and I habitually used was in the shop and I had gone to Atlanta in an unmarked narcotics car.

And now I will tell you a story.

The Henry County Line

Henry County is just south of Atlanta. Henry County has a reputation for enforcing its speed laws very, very thoroughly. Now mind, it's not a speed trap; all speed limit markers are appropriately and reasonably displayed, and fines are fair—but Henry County does enforce its speed laws. Eighteen-wheelers going from Miami to Atlanta or vice versa drive sixty-five or seventy most of the way; but when they cross the Henry County line they pull up their skirts and tippytoe across it at fifty-five, and they stay at fifty-five all the way through Henry County and floorboard it again as soon as they cross the line on the other side.

On the way home from the crime lab, I simultaneously became aware of three things: (1) I was in Henry County; (2) there was a deputy sheriff's car parked on the side of the road just in front of me; and (3) I was doing ninety-five.

It was, of course, far too late to slow down. I zipped on past the deputy, wondering what I was going say when I had to call Colonel Denney (the chief of detectives) to come to Henry County and get me out of jail. But the deputy didn't try to stop me. I suppose he figured that anybody doing ninety-five through Henry County in a car with four whip antennas had to be a police officer on official business—which I was, but I didn't have to be going that fast.

This has nothing to do with identifying the corpse, who turned out—when scientists developed fingerprints from his dermis—to be wearing his own belt buckle, but it is part of the whole story.

And now you know what happened with the Jackson Street Corpse. Even that identification was relatively easy—the man was, after all, found in the backyard of the house where he had been living, there were only three possibles, and his dermis was relatively intact.

Nothing at All to Go On

Corpses—even skeletons—are found with far less to go on than that.

Ultimately, of course, before anybody can be identified, there must be a possible person to check out. This "possible identification" may come from missing person reports, from a killer's ten-years-late confession, from citizens who call police after publication of a description. If we have no fingerprints, where do we go?

Ear-Print Identification

Believe it or not, a person can be identified by his/her ears, if there is an adequate side photo that shows the ear clearly and if the ear is intact. Scientists have found that the creases and lines in the ear lobe, as well as the arrangement of the entire outer structure in the ear, are consistent and unduplicated, although the creases do tend to become considerably deeper with age. Once, at an ident convention, I talked with a man who told me he'd identified a safecracker by the ear print he left on the door of the safe.

This knowledge could have saved an English author considerable embarrassment in the early 1980s. The author—whose name I will withhold out of courtesy—became obsessed with the notion that the man in Lee Harvey Oswald's grave was not Oswald, the presumed assassin of President John F. Kennedy, but rather a "ringer" who had been substituted for the real Oswald after Oswald left for the Soviet Union. He insisted that the fingerprint identification, from Oswald's Marine Corps fingerprints and Dallas Police Department fingerprints, was no good because in his opinion someone had substituted the "ringer's" prints for the prints of the real Oswald in the Marine Corps files. He spent considerable time, money and agitation demanding that the grave be opened; the Fort Worth *Star-Telegram*, which I read at the time, was following the story in considerable detail.

I wrote a polite letter to the reporter covering the story, asking him to let the writer know that opening the grave was not necessary. There were good photographs in existence of Oswald both before and after the trip to the U.S.S.R.; if the writer feared Marine Corps photos had been tampered with, that was all right, because there were also family photos of Oswald. I had seen enough to know that there were clear photographs showing the ears. I suggested he simply get an ear examiner to examine the photographs and that would give him his conclusive answer without the trouble and expense of opening a grave.

The reporter told me he had passed the information along.

The writer ignored me.

If I recall correctly, he eventually did get the grave opened.

Surprise, surprise. The body in the grave was that of Lee Harvey Oswald. I do not know on what basis the conclusion was reached, as the writer had already declared the fingerprints inconclusive.

But there are other ways of identifying a body.

Let's go to a new chapter for them.

TABLE 6
Finding Reference Sources

The more technically complicated your writing is, the more critical it is to find plenty of reference material. But that can be hard to do. Here are some hints that might help:

- Use more than one encyclopedia. Different encyclopedias look at material differently; therefore, one may provide information that another omits. I generally consult *World Book* and *Encyclopaedia Britannica*. You'll decide on your own favorites on the basis of what you need and what's available.

- At the end of each encyclopedia article is a list of related topics. Look them up also, as one of them might tell just what you need to know.

- Unless you live in a very large city, you may need to make a special trip to the closest big-city and/or university library. At times I have consulted as many as five different libraries in the course of one book. Jean Auel, who spends years researching her Earth's Children books, would probably consider me to be scarcely scratching the surface.

- Ask a librarian to help you. Most of us are aware of only one serial bibliography, *The Reader's Guide to Periodical Literature*. Librarians know of hundreds of serial bibliographies. Some of them are specialized and might be looking at your specific topic. In addition, there are many computerized data bases in larger libraries. Some of those may charge a fee, but others are paid for by your tax dollars.

- Learn to use the appropriate guides to topic headings in card or computerized library book catalogs. If you can't find anything on your topic, you might be looking under the wrong headings. The librarian can help you find the right ones.

- When you find a useful book, inspect its bibliography. Almost certainly it will list other books and articles that will be helpful.

- Use interlibrary loan. If a source is not in your library, your librarian can order it for your temporary use. You will pay no more than the cost of mailing; quite often there is no charge.

- As you build your professional library, haunt used bookstores, Goodwill stores, Salvation Army stores, and Deseret Industries stores. On many topics, used books—even old books—are as useful as new books.

- Learn for yourself as many as you reasonably can of the skills your series character or your "big book" character possesses. There are adult education classes available almost everywhere, and they're generally quite inexpensive. Nobody expects you to spend ten years in medical school and internships before you write a novel about a brain surgeon, but learning to fire a pistol, perhaps to ski if your heroine likes to ski or garden if your hero likes to garden, is easy enough. In fiction as elsewhere, no authority speaks more loudly than the voice of experience.

MORE ON IDENTIFYING HUMAN REMAINS

The head is cut off, the brain removed and several deep cuts made in the back and sides of the head; it is then placed in pure running water. In twelve hours' time the green colouring of the skin of the face will for the most part have disappeared or have got blanched, and the swelling greatly diminished; the top of the skull is then replaced and the skin of the head sewn up again. The head is then plunged into a concentrated solution of alcohol. After another twelve hours the green colouring and the swelling of decomposition will have so completely disappeared that the face will finally assume its normal condition and present the appearance of a corpse newly embalmed. Instead of the above solution, chloride of zinc may be employed with equal success. Of course the possibility of reconstructing a face has its limits, especially when the hair has already fallen off and the skin of the face begun to be perforated with holes — in such a case nothing can be done.

—Hans Gross,
Criminal Investigation

To the best of my knowledge, the method detailed here by Gross to make a decaying face recognizable is no longer in use anywhere in the world; furthermore, in my personal library of criminology, and in all the criminology books I have read from many other libraries in several states, I have never found an example in which this method was used for identification.

But some other methods are equally interesting, and almost as bizarre.

Forensic Dentistry

There are very few full-time forensic dentists; more often a forensic dentist is a regular dentist who has become interested in forensic dentistry and offered his services to the local police department. And yet forensic dentistry can do marvelous things. The best fictional account of it I've come across occurs in a Lord Peter Wimsey story, "In the Teeth of the Evidence," by Dorothy Sayers. In that story, what at first appears to be an innocent dentist, accidentally burned to death in a fire in his garage, turns out to be a transient murdered by a felonious dentist attempting to escape a very bad situation.

The story is interesting because Mr. Prendergast, the apparent victim, anticipates that a dental investigation will be made of the corpse, and he carefully re-creates his own dental chart in the transient's mouth. But he's caught when Mr. Lamplough, Lord Peter's dentist who assists the police, discovers that what is supposed to be a fused porcelain filling inserted in 1923 is in fact a cast porcelain filling, and the process was not invented until 1928.

This discovery meant that the body was not that of a dentist who had accidentally burned to death in a fire in his garage, but a victim murdered by a felonious dentist.

But how is a dental identification done?

The dental chart in Figure 7-1, used by permission of the dental patient and his dentist, is the latest thing in dental-chart technology. Rather than a paper chart to update periodically, which may become frayed and yellowed over time or even lost in inadvertent file shuffling, this chart was stored on computer. When the patient asked for a photocopy of his chart for use in this book, the dentist assured him what he would get would be even better than a photocopy: an original computer printout of all work done in this patient's mouth to date. But basically, whether it is computerized or done on paper, this is what any dental chart done in the last hundred or so years will look like.

A dentist working on any patient—whether s/he has worked with this forty-one-year-old patient for forty years or has just encountered this eighty-year-old patient for the first time—charts not only his/her own work but also all work already present before the first time this dentist examined this patient. The printed chart form to be filled in by hand, or the computer form, shows all teeth normally present in an adult; the dentist notes on the chart which teeth are absent in this patient, which teeth have work, where the work is, and what kind of work was done. A dental chart, if accurate, is almost as conclusive as fingerprints. Therefore, if the jaws of an unknown corpse are compared with the dental chart of the person the corpse is likely to be, and if the location and type of dental work

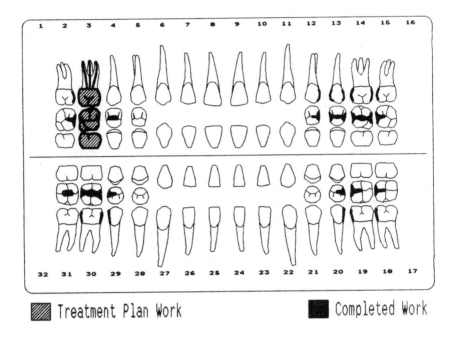

▨ Treatment Plan Work ■ Completed Work

Figure 7-1. A sample dental chart.

match the chart, then presumptive evidence exists that this corpse is the person for whom that chart was made.

X rays, if they exist, will supplement material available on the chart. But unless full-mouth X rays exist, an X ray may show too small an area with too few identification points to make a full identification possible from X ray alone. The dental charts are normally essential.

But there are possible problems. Of course, if someone actually intends to substitute a body for a known person, the body must first fit the general description of the person. Even a fire will not make it impossible to distinguish between a six-foot-tall man and a five-foot-tall woman. Then a dentist—or at least a highly knowledgeable dental technician who could not practice on a living person but might be able to do fairly convincing work on a corpse—must be willing to spend a lot of time doing dental work on a corpse, and that dentist or technician must have the original chart available to work from.

In fact, fraud of this sort is probably more common in fiction than in real life. The coincidence of an available unknown corpse to be substituted for a living person and a dentist willing to commit that sort of fraud is rare. But other problems can occur.

First, if the corpse is reduced to skeletal remains, some of the teeth may be lost. The teeth are not likely to decay—in fact, in a person who before death was healthy, the teeth will probably be the very last items to decay. If you have ever—as I once did in childhood—found a coyote skull and tried to extract its teeth, you know how extremely difficult it is. But as the skeleton continues to weather, perhaps to be gnawed on by predators, teeth may be lost from the jaws and hauled away by predators or washed away by heavy rains. Poor health or borderline scurvy (which loosens teeth and is extremely common in the homeless, drug abusers or other malnourished people) increases the incidence of lost teeth. If the people collecting the skeletal remains are not extremely careful with sieving, teeth may be left behind.

Sieving

Sieving, an archaeological technique adapted to forensic medicine, consists of putting all dirt removed from the area of a find through a fairly fine sieve and then sorting everything caught by the mesh, discarding rocks and so forth and retaining everything of potential evidential value. Frequently, in criminalistic work as in archaeological work, sieving turns up small items of great potential — sometimes teeth.

Second, the charts may not be completely accurate. The person might have gone to another dentist later, after the dentist the family knew about, and had more dental work done, so that a too-early dental chart is compared. If the later work did not obscure the earlier work, identification may still be possible, but if later work covered earlier work — e.g., what was a small amalgam filling is now a deep root canal; teeth that were filled are now missing — identification may become impossible.

And there are other reasons why charts may not be completely accurate. Rarely, dentists lie to their patients about how much work they've done. Christopher Joyce and Eric Stover, in *Witnesses From the Grave: The Stories Bones Tell*, quote Robert Kirschner, assistant medical examiner for Cook County, Illinois. He'd been working on identifying bodies from an airplane crash and referred to a very well-dressed young woman who'd had quite a lot of dental work done:

> "It was very difficult to get records from her dentist. . . ." When they finally got hold of the records, it was obvious why the dentist had been reluctant: the records showed far less work than what the team found in the woman's teeth. "[H]e had obviously shown half of his dental work on his records so he could cut his income to the IRS. On the other hand, if you got a welfare dentist, you saw a person who actually has three fillings in their mouth, but the dental records would show ten. They were marking 'em down left and right so they could collect from Medicaid."
>
> (101)

This section, quoted in the the *Wall Street Journal*'s review of the book, illustrates one major problem. Try to make a positive identification from charts like those. It can't be done — unless the dentist has some sort of code to show what work s/he *really* did and is willing to admit it.

Age may also be a factor. If the last time this person went to the dentist was at the age of eight, and the person is now sixteen or seventeen, the chart cannot possibly be accurate. Too many deciduous teeth have been replaced by permanent teeth, which might have come in at a different angle from the baby teeth and will certainly have different problems.

Forensic dentistry has uses other than identifying corpses. In one case, a burglar who took one bite out of an apple and then left the apple at the scene was later definitely identified — after a suspect had been produced in other ways — by a cast of his teeth, which matched a cast of the bite taken from the apple. In a far more serious case, in which a murder victim had been repeatedly bitten, tooth marks identified the killer. Obviously, a nonsuspect ident in this type of case is impossible; the suspect must first be produced by other means of investigation.

Long-Bone X Rays

If for any reason both fingerprints and dental charts are unfeasible — e.g., the corpse had dentures (which are missing) and no hands; somebody has made a determined effort to avoid identification by removing head, hands and feet — the next step, if long-bone X rays of the suspected person exist, is long-bone X-ray comparison. Of course, the more X rays are available of arms and legs, the surer the identification is; however, a very detailed X ray of even one leg or one arm may be sufficient for a firm identification.

Dealing With Skeletal Remains

When working with unknown remains, investigators follow a protocol, apparently developed at the time of the Parkman-Webster case, when one medical school professor murdered another and was convicted on testimony from the janitor (see discussion of this case later in this chapter).

Briefly, the protocol asks medical experts to determine as much as possible about the remains, beginning with the broadest category (human or animal? one person or several?) and gradually narrowing to age, sex, anomalies that might be used for identification, and finally focusing in on time (as narrowly as possible, realizing at times determining the century might be the best possible) and cause of death, if it can be determined. For a more detailed explanation of the protocol, see Joyce and Stover, pp. 52ff.

Obviously, the more there is left, the more likely these questions are to be answerable. Working with a skull alone, even the best pathologist is likely to mistake the sex as often as 25 percent of the time; and as races become more and more mixed through interracial marriage and other interracial sexual contact, it becomes less and less possible to distinguish race. If the entire skeleton is present, handedness is easy to determine, because the right-handed person's right arm tends to be slightly larger and vice versa (apparently because of more use rather than of anything innate). Sex in an adult is fairly easy to determine if pelvic bones are present, but even then there is as much as a 10 percent chance of error. Sex in child skeletal remains is extremely difficult, as before puberty there is very little difference. If the long bones remain, height is fairly easy to determine. Weight may be somewhat more difficult, particularly if the person was extremely overweight.

Cause of death in skeletal remains may be easy to determine, if a bullet, knife or arrowhead remains in the area, or if marks where a bullet ricocheted off a rib are visible, or if the bones themselves are visibly damaged. But soft-tissue damage will be impossible to recognize in a skeleton.

What this means to you is that in your writing, you may determine how much is left of the decedent and how much your fictional pathologist will be able to determine from the remains.

Reconstructing the Face

If you can find an English translation of I.A. Gerasimov's *The Face Finder*, it's well worth reading. Gerasimov, a forensic anthropologist working in Moscow, is capable of reconstructing the face from the skull. He has determined that the ways that muscles attach to the skull can be used to figure out depth of tissue at different places on the face, thus overcoming the problem of determining the person's probable facial fullness. If this problem is difficult to envision, think of someone you know who has recently gained, or lost, quite a lot of weight. Could you be certain of recognizing an extremely heavy person from a reconstruction of what that person's face would look like if the person were slim? With some people, there is little problem, but most of us have had the experience I had when I was nineteen—encountering a friend who had graduated a year before I did. She had been heavy all the way through school, but after graduation she moved away and embarked on a long-range weight-loss program. Two years later, when she and I met, she had to introduce herself—I hadn't the slightest idea who she was. Her slim face could not be recognized from her heavy face.

Gerasimov has worked in many criminal cases; he's also been involved in reconstructing the faces of historical figures whose skulls could be recovered and of whom authentic portraits are not known. The photographs in his book of facial reconstructions of such people as Ivan the Terrible and Attila the Hun are fascinating and at times extremely revealing.

Martin Cruz Smith's novel *Gorky Park* was based on the work of Gerasimov, and the description Smith gave of Gerasimov's work is far more detailed than this book has the space to present. Smith wrote the book partly under the assumption that no one else in the world was doing the same sort of work. This fact, to him, meant that he had to travel to the Soviet Union to do research, and had to set the book in the Soviet Union. What began, in his mind, as another mystery of the type he was already writing turned into a personal and fictional odyssey. The book, which took more than seven years to write, catapulted the writer from the status of barely making a living (among other things, he had worked as an ice cream man) to the status of millionaire.

And there's one very interesting thing I thought you'd like to know: Smith was incorrect in his assumption that nobody but Gerasimov was reconstructing faces from skulls. William Krogman of the FBI was one of the pioneers of the technique, and the Oklahoma team of Clyde Snow and Betty Gatliff work all over the world. Similar work, using photos as well as sculpture, has been going on in England for more than fifty years. Which brings to mind an interesting question: If he'd known the truth, would he have ever written *Gorky Park*? Well, if you've read *Gorky Park*, most likely you, like me, are glad Smith knew about Gerasimov's cases but not, perhaps, about Buck Ruxton.

Though to be completely fair, I should add that Smith might have known about the Buck Ruxton case but decided it was immaterial. The techniques used were somewhat different.

Who Was Buck Ruxton?

A Parsi, he was born Bukhtyar Sustomji Ratanji Hakim. His medical training was in Bombay, but when he moved to England, he

Anglicized his name. In 1928, at the age of thirty, he entered into a common-law marriage with Isabella Van Ess, and by 1930, the Ruxtons were settled in Lancaster.

The marriage was a stormy one. According to later reports, Ruxton was convinced his wife was cheating on him; Mrs. Ruxton several times reported to police that he was physically abusing her. In 1935, Mrs. Ruxton and her twenty-year-old maid Mary Rogerson were reported missing. Ruxton maintained that his wife had left him for another man; he had no explanation for why the maid also was missing. His explanations of the blood on carpeting and clothing also were somewhat frail.

In late September of 1935, portions of two bodies were found in and near the Annan River between Carlisle and Edinburgh. All identifying characteristics, including fingertips, eyes, and front teeth, had been removed. There is a slight possibility that they might not have been connected with Mrs. Ruxton and Miss Rogerson, except that portions of the body were wrapped in a copy of a newspaper sold only in Lancaster and nearby More-cambe.

When questioned, Ruxton continued to insist that his wife had left him and he didn't know what had happened to the maid. But the circumstances were suspicious: Mrs. Ruxton had buck teeth, and the teeth of the older woman were missing. Miss Rogerson had a squint in one eye, and the eyes of the younger woman were missing. And there was still all that blood on the carpet.

Pathologists from the universities in Edinburgh and Glasgow examined the bodies. Enough was left of the dermis to permit a fingerprint examination of Miss Rogerson. To identify the other body, pathologists seized photographs of Mrs. Ruxton. Then, from the same angle, they photographed the unknown skull. The two photographs were then superimposed and rephotographed. The fit was perfect.

Was the body indeed that of Mrs. Ruxton? Was Dr. Buck Ruxton guilty of murder? The question was for a jury to decide. Ruxton continued to deny everything, calling his accusation "absolute bunkum" (Gaute and Odell 200). The jury did decide; Ruxton was hanged on May 12, 1936, at Strangeways Prison. It was later revealed that he had written and signed a brief confession on October 14, only one day after his arrest.

Strange Identifications

In some situations, positive identification may be impossible, but because of surrounding circumstances, a presumptive identification that will be sufficient grounds for a murder charge may be made. John Haigh, English murderer of the year in 1949, misunderstanding the meaning of the term *corpus delicti*, dissolved the body of his victim Olive Durand-Deacon in forty gallons of sulphuric acid. Her dentist's identification of her plastic denture (still intact) coupled with other evidence was sufficient to lead to his conviction and his execution on August 10, 1949, in Wandsworth Prison. Numerous books have been written about this case, which is considered one of the classics of criminology.

Similarly, on December 21, 1957, con man L. Ewing Scott was convicted in Los Angeles, California, of the murder of his wife Evelyn on or about May 16, 1955, even though all that was ever found of her was her denture and some of her medicine, both dumped near the incinerator of the Scotts' next-door neighbors. A fascinating book, *Corpus Delicti*, by Diane Wagner, details this case and the painstaking investigation that led to Scott's conviction.

The Parkman-Webster Case

And there is the one that has been called "America's classic murder." It happened in staid Boston, in November 1849. Dr. John White Webster of the Massachusetts Medical College, a Harvard graduate, owed money to Dr. John Parkman, another professor at the medical college. When Dr. Parkman tried to collect, Dr. Webster knocked him in the head with a stick of kindling wood . . . and who knows better how to dispose of a body than a doctor?

Webster dissected Parkman's body and burned the pieces in his assay oven. He probably would have gotten away with it except for Ephraim Littlefield, the college janitor, who remembered how hot the wall got behind the oven the day Dr. Parkman vanished. Webster got nervous; he gave the janitor a turkey for a Thanksgiving present. But he had not been noted for generosity to the help, and that only made Littlefield more suspicious. Finally Littlefield, knowing that for a janitor to accuse a professor without evidence would be futile, pried out some brick and found portions of a body. Now he had something to tell the police.

Webster, of course, insisted the body portions were from a cadaver he'd been working on. But even Webster's imagination could not dream up a reply when police found Parkman's teeth in Webster's assay oven. And one professor was hanged on August 30, 1850, for bludgeoning to death another professor, with a conviction based on the testimony of the janitor . . . not quite what you'd expect in Boston in the mid-nineteenth century.

How do we know so much about what actually happened?

Just prior to his execution, Webster confessed.

What Is a Corpus Delicti?

More than a few murderers have come to grief because of their misunderstanding of this legal term. Knowing that a case cannot be tried without a *corpus delicti*, and seeing the word *corpus*, which is so similar to *corpse*, they leap to the conclusion that nobody can be tried for murder if the corpse cannot be located or identified.

And indeed the word *corpus* does mean *body*, but the reference is to the *body of evidence*, not to the body of the victim. Which, for example, was how that shy little dentist Dr. Hawley Harvey Crippen happened to be hanged in 1910 for the murder of his truly appalling wife, would-be singer Belle Elmore (stage name) who had married him using the name of Cora Turner. (Her real name was Kunigunde Mackamotzki, and I mention this only because it seems more fitting. Photographs indicate she had the build of the stereotypical operatic fat lady; reviews indicate she did not possess a matching talent.)

Crippen earned the living. Did the housework. Indulged Belle in jewelry and furs. Paid for Belle's ill-fated forays onto the stage; critics described her music as screeching. Was openly taunted by Belle and her fashionable friends. Finally fell in love with his shy secretary, Ethel le Neve.

When Crippen told his friends Belle had returned to the United States, but none of her friends heard from her, that looked odd enough. But when Ethel first moved in and then was seen wearing Belle's furs and jewelry, Belle's fashionable friends got suspicious.

Police inspector Walter Dew of Scotland Yard investigated, found nothing amiss. But Crippen panicked and fled, headed for Canada on the *SS Montrose*, taking Ethel with him disguised (not very convincingly) as a boy. Dew investigated further. Body parts were found buried in the cellar, but the head, skeleton and limbs were gone. Belle was identified on the basis of a surgery scar and a vest (according to some accounts, a pajama shirt); Dew boarded a faster ship and arrested the two on July 31, 1910; and Crippen learned what *corpus delicti* really meant. Nobody believed the defense insistence that the body remains were somebody other than Belle and the scar was really a skin crease. What would somebody else's remains be doing wrapped in Cora Crippen's vest or pajama shirt as the case may be?

Many books have been written about this case. A careful reader can find it easy to be a little sorry for Crippen . . . but I do wish that before he died, he had explained how he disposed of the rest of the body.

And then there was Edward Ball, who was convicted in 1936 in County Dublin, Ireland, of the murder of his mother, although no body was ever found. The *corpus delicti* included an abandoned automobile, bloodstained towels, bloodstained clothing, bloodstained carpet and a bloodstained hatchet. Although the defense insisted that Mrs. Vera Ball, estranged wife of a physician, had committed suicide, the prosecution evidence was overwhelming.

Perhaps the most interesting *corpus delicti* case was that of James Camb, a ship's steward who was convicted in March 1948 of the strangulation murder of Eileen Isabella Gibson, an actress whose stage name was Gay Gibson. Strong evidence was presented that Camb had attempted to sexually assault Gibson; had strangled her when she attempted to ring for help; had covered up her attempt to call for help by pretending, when the ship's night watchman arrived in answer to her bell, that he had arrived sooner; and then had pushed the body through the porthole. He eventually admitted having sex with her and pushing her through the porthole, but he contended she had died naturally, apparently of a heart attack or a "fit"; that he had attempted artificial respiration; and then, panicking, he put the body through the porthole. But that did not explain the scratches on his hands and wrists apparently made by the woman fighting for her life, nor did it explain the ringing of the signal bell from her stateroom the night she vanished. The prosecution contended—successfully—that Camb had disposed of the body under the all-too-common assumption that he could not be convicted of murder if the body could not be found.

Like many other people who made the same assumption, he was proven wrong.

DNA fingerprinting, if available then, could have provided

conclusive proof in the case of Crippen and of Webster, if—that is—known genetic material of Belle Elmore and of Dr. Parkman had existed. It wouldn't have helped in the case of Ball, because nobody argued that the blood was not that of Mrs. Ball or that Mr. Ball had not disposed of his mother's body; the question rather was one of how Mrs. Ball came to be a body; nor would it have helped in the Camb case, as no one disputed that the body fluids in the bed were those of Gay Gibson. In the Haigh case, it probably wouldn't have helped; and in the Scott case, it certainly wouldn't have.

But we're just now on the cutting edge of DNA experimentation, and what will be possible twenty years from now none of us can begin to guess. So let's think, now, about the gene test that can—at least theoretically—prove conclusive identity.

Well, almost conclusive. Although in general DNA fingerprinting can distinguish between siblings, Jay Henry of the Utah State Crime Laboratory pointed out to me that it cannot distinguish between identical twins, as they would, of course, have the same DNA material—that is, the same genetic heritage

The technique called DNA fingerprinting—the name was coined by Sue Jeffreys, wife of English scientist Alec Jeffreys, who invented the process—is the descendant of a long line of work. But what does it mean?

DNA Fingerprinting

When I was in junior high, I was taught that human beings have forty-eight pairs of chromosomes in every cell of their bodies except reproductive cells, each chromosome consisting of a long string of genes. That was not quite correct; scientists had miscounted, and we now know that human beings have forty-six pairs of chromosomes. These strings were originally called chromosomes because, under extreme magnification, they look extremely colorful (the prefix *chrome* refers to color). The genes are composed of spiral-twisted strands of deoxyribonucleic acid, the chemical that carries the computer codes, so to speak, that tell the body how to develop not only in humans but in all animal and plant life.

Now bear with me a minute, because if you're up on your biology you know all this. Here's where you get these sets of chromosomes: the reproductive cells, unlike all other cells, have single chromosomes rather than pairs. When the spermatozoa, the male reproductive cell, and the ovum, the female reproductive cell, join, the first thing they do is produce a *zygote*, a new cell that joins the single chromosomes from the ovum and the single chromosomes from the spermatozoa to produce new pairs of chromosomes. So each human being is produced by a code that comes half from the father and half from the mother.

Now, if exactly the same chromosomes from each pair went into each ovum or into each spermatozoa, all the offspring of one set of parents would be just alike. But in fact, either chromosome from each pair can go into each ovum or spermatozoa; furthermore, genes possess the ability to "jump" from one chromosome to another, so that a chromosome that came mainly from a person's father may contain genes that came from a person's mother. As each human chromosome contains about a hundred thousand genes, this means effectively that the genetic heritage in each zygote is going to be different from the genetic heritage in any other zygote. And as that zygote turns into a fetus, which turns into a human being, each human being—again with the exception of identical twins or other identical multiples, who develop from a single zygote—every human being is going to have a different set of DNA from every other human being.

This means many things. First, it is possible to identify an individual from very small samplings once a suspect has been developed by other means. That handful of hair the victim snatched, the scrapings under the fingernails where the victim scratched the assailant, the blood where the assailant got a nosebleed—even the semen left behind by the rapist—all these can be matched to the individual they belong to.

Earl Ubell, writing in *Parade* magazine, told of the first case solved by Jeffreys's method: A man suspected of the rape and murder of two fifteen-year-old girls was innocent; the semen stains on the bodies did not match his DNA. Police then asked for blood samples from all the men living in the neighborhood. Obviously, the men could not be required to give these samples, but their failure to do so might raise certain questions in the mind of investigators. One man asked a friend to provide a blood sample in his place. That naturally roused the curiosity of the friend and hence of the police, and court orders were eventually obtained. When the DNA of the suspect, Colin Pitchfork, was compared to the semen, it matched.

There are other uses for DNA fingerprinting. In questions of paternity, it is possible to prove with very close certainty who is and is not the parent of the child in question. In one very sad case, it was able to show that parents had left the hospital with each other's baby, but by the time the switch was discovered one girl was ten years old and one girl was dead. Another time, British authorities thought that a citizen of Ghana was trying to enter England on a passport owned by a resident of Ghana with British citizenship. DNA fingerprinting of both parents and of the young man proved that the young man was exactly who he said he was; half his DNA had clearly come from his purported mother and half from his purported father.

In 1991, scientists proposed opening Abraham Lincoln's tomb and obtaining genetic scrapings in order to check for the Marfan's syndrome gene and finally determine for sure whether Lincoln did indeed have Marfan's syndrome.

What Is Marfan's Syndrome?

Marfan's syndrome is a hereditary ailment of the long bones, connective tissue and blood vessels. The most obvious symptom externally is very long legs and arms; the most serious symptom is a tendency toward spontaneous rupture of the aorta, the largest blood vessel in the body, and as a result Marfan's victims rarely live past middle age without surgical intervention. Modern medical historians, examining Lincoln's portraits and what is known now about his body measurements (easily determined, as some of his clothing still exists) insist he was a Marfan's victim. Other historians aren't so sure.

Marfan's syndrome may be useful in fiction because a rupture of the aorta is excruciatingly painful, and although the victim will usually bleed to death internally within ten minutes, it has happened that a victim, bleeding internally and in great pain, has grabbed a pistol and shot himself (in this case, rarely herself). In that case, for insurance purposes, the question of whether the person died from suicide or from the ruptured aorta may become crucial.

And of course, if someone else muddies the water further by taking away the pistol . . . there's a lot you can do with that.

But DNA fingerprinting is not yet fully accepted. So far, more than 400 cases have gone to trial, and no one knows how many cases have been settled without trial because DNA evidence was available. But in a nonbinding precedent, Judge Douglas Keddie of Yuma County, Arizona, ruled that DNA tests were not yet acceptable in his court, despite the contentions of the FBI agents who had performed it that the test was conclusive. According to Judge Keddie, the fact that the test is supposedly so conclusive means that it "puts a fist on the scale of justice." Because it is "so likely to sway a jury, it must be subjected to the strictest scrutiny" (Kolata).

And Kolata to a large degree is right. In a copyrighted article originally published in the *Washington Post*, Boyce Rensberger pointed out some of the problems with DNA fingerprinting. In general if a complete DNA fingerprint is taken, all people except identical siblings can be distinguished from one another. But the problem is that DNA fingerprinting does not look at the entire DNA sequence; rather, it looks at certain parts of sequences that are normally different in all people. Given this short sequence comparison, it is indeed true that any person is totally different from any person not closely related. But the chances that two siblings will be identical in this short-sequence comparison may be as low as 1 in 128.

Furthermore, Rensberger quoted geneticists Richard Lewontin of Harvard University and Daniel Hartl of Washington University as saying it is possible that the odds for and against a wrong match must be calculated differently for each race and ethnic group and subgroup, because some ethnic groups are more interbred than others.

This can be as important in writing fiction as in real life; I'm already thinking of ways of using it, and I'm sure you can think of many more.

One more thing . . . don't have a DNA test performed in the morning and the results announced that afternoon. DNA test results require an absolute minimum of ten days, but two weeks is more likely.

What is the future of identification?

Genetic fingerprinting—when the entire genetic sequence, rather than only a part of it, is used—is probably as good as it gets, though the techniques of genetic fingerprinting and of interpreting the tests will certainly be improved in the future. At present, the tests involve several complicated chemical steps, and the resultant printout resembles a bar-code of the type used in grocery stores to scan prices, except that it is far more complicated and far more colorful.

Scientists in several parts of the world are involved in a project called gene-mapping. They hope that by the time the project is completed, around the turn of the century, they will know what every gene on every chromosome controls. Frequently the papers announce new discoveries related to this mapping; within the time I have been working on this book I've read about the discovery of the location of genes that relate to several different kinds of cancer and of genes that may control the onset of Alzheimer's disease, and of course it was the gene-mapping project that located the Marfan's syndrome gene. Once this project is complete, DNA fingerprinting will be able not only to identify a person, but also perhaps to determine what illnesses that person is likely to have in his/her lifetime and maybe even what his probable appearance, intelligence and talents are.

I've already mentioned that the U.S. military services are now storing a small amount of genetic material of each recruit, so that in the future there will be no more unknown soldiers. What else? The sky's the limit; I would certainly expect that in the near future, DNA codes will be stored on all known sex criminals, and it may well be that within the next hundred years, DNA codes will be automatically stored at the time of birth of every individual. Try to get away with changing your identity — or disguising the corpse of your victim — then!

TABLE 7

Cost and Value of Different Means of Identification

Means of Identification	Ease	Cost	Accuracy
visual recognition	high	low	variable*
fingerprints	high	low	high
long bone X rays	moderate	moderate	variable
dental	moderate	low	variable
DNA	low	high	high
birthmarks	moderate	low	very low
footprints	moderate	low	variable**
palm prints	high	low	high
scars	moderate	low	very low
tattoos	moderate	low	very low

*Most people have doubles. I thought nobody in the world looked like me, until my middle daughter saw a coworker's mother. Keep looking. You'll find your double. Visual recognition is normally accurate, if the corpse is well-known to the person making the identification and in good condition, and there is no possible reason for a substitution.

**Footprints, if properly taken, are as evidential as fingerprints and palm prints. Flexion creases can be as identifiable as ridge details. Unfortunately, most hospital footprints of babies are cute, fuzzy and illegible.

THE AUTOPSY AND AFTER

Of all the experts an Investigating Officer has to deal with the most important and the most frequently questioned are the medical jurisprudents; with them therefore the Investigating Officer should enter into very intimate relations. . . . If . . .they have zeal and energy, working together will encourage their efforts, and their collaboration will considerably aid the solution of the problem.

—Hans Gross,
Criminal Investigation

At present, the Tokyo Police Department leads the world in applying new scientific techniques to criminal investigation; the Federal Bureau of Investigation, Scotland Yard, the New York Police Department and the Los Angeles Police Department all run very close seconds. Beyond them, as close thirds, are many city, state and national police departments, as new discoveries are written up in journals and quickly shared with other departments. This chapter views the autopsy from the point of view of the investigator. For the pathologist's point of view, see Keith Wilson's *Cause of Death* (Writer's Digest Books, 1992).

The Importance of the Autopsy

Gross emphasized the importance of a good working relationship between criminal investigators and medical examiners, and that situation has not changed in the slightest. A good medical examiner can help to guide the investigation in the right direction; a bad one can throw it off track completely. But even a good one, if s/he is uncomfortable working with the police, can cause problems.

During the time I was policing in Albany, Georgia, we had—for a while—two medical examiners working simultaneously. One, though an extremely competent board-certified pathologist, felt very uncomfortable working with police; the other, though not yet board-certified, enjoyed his relation with us. Guess which one we preferred to work with?

If you remember the television show "Quincy," which was about a Los Angeles medical examiner, you undoubtedly were amused by the opening sequence of every episode, which showed a group of police officers trying to watch an autopsy and, one by one, falling over backward. I never did that, though I will admit that I spent my first autopsy sitting on the floor because I was afraid that if I stood up, I would fall over. It's not the sight that tends to bother most people, but the smell, which can best be described as a mixture of too-raw flesh, human mortality (which you may not realize has an odor until you work around it), and body odors including urine, feces and blood.

Why would police need to view an autopsy anyway? (A Fort Worth pathologist told me he prefers "postmortem examination" because, he insists, *autopsy* literally means surgery on oneself. The dictionaries do not agree, and the word *autopsy* seems to be the most common one.) There are several reasons for police to see autopsies. For one thing, if evidence must be collected during the autopsy, having the police officer on hand to receive the evidence directly shortens the chain of custody and reduces the amount of time a busy pathologist has to spend in court. (Busy police officers' time is considered less important.) Second, if the police officer is on hand, police will have access to information much sooner than if they have to wait for the official autopsy report, which may take several days to several weeks. But most important, if the officer is present to ask questions, information may come out which would not find its way into a formal autopsy report, and which might be extremely important. (I must point out that, during that disastrous first autopsy, I did stay in the room, albeit on the floor—a twenty-year veteran police officer who had entered with me stayed only five minutes before going out the door with his hands over his mouth.)

I eventually grew to find autopsies very interesting, especially when "little Santos" was doing the job. Dr. Santos seemed a born teacher; he really enjoyed not only explaining to me what he had found, but also insisting that I look more closely until I could see the same thing. On one occasion, he pulled out the entire digestive tract of the cadaver and laid it out on the table to explain to me how digestion works. I could have understood that a little better if the victim had died of poisoning—in fact, she had been the victim of a simple bashing—but nonetheless, it was extremely informative.

I remember two other autopsies particularly vividly. In one, we had a strangulation murder. We suspected strangulation with some sort of ligature, as there were no hand-shaped bruises on the neck, and there were many creases in the skin, any one of which could have hidden the marks of a ligature. But when Dr. Santos laid open the skin of the neck, he was able to show me, on layers of flesh inside the skin, very deep bluish-purple hand marks. The victim had been manually strangled by someone whose hands were quite large, and the creases on the neck were all just creases.

The other was one of the most horrible cases I ever saw. It actually happened outside our normal jurisdiction, but our evidence collection facilities were far better than those of the jurisdiction where the crime took place, and Butch and I were called out on it. Doc was unavailable; I think he was on leave.

The victim, a young housewife, had been sexually assaulted and stabbed more than a hundred times. The first attack apparently took place in the kitchen; most of the stabbing was in the laundry room; and then, the best we could determine, the murderer had stood and watched while the mortally wounded victim crawled down the hall toward her bedroom, trying to reach a telephone to call for help.

After Butch, some local officers, and I worked the crime scene the rest of the day the body was found, Butch and I went to the autopsy. Butch had never seen one before. All three of us—Dr. Santos, Butch and I—were never able to figure out exactly how many stab wounds there were, as there were places where the knife had repeatedly entered the same wound. Dr. Santos found at least four wounds that would have been fatal within minutes. And he found one thing that helped, later, to pin the crime on the right person: He found that the knife blade was short and either slightly serrated or very dull. (It turned out to be the latter.)

Here's what Butch and I were proudest of about that case: The day after we finished the crime scene, the head of the state crime lab flew down to do everything we had missed. He went out to the scene, viewed it, and then said there was nothing left for him to do. Butch and I had done it all. And he got in his plane and flew back to Atlanta.

What are some of the things that can be determined from an autopsy? What are some of the things that cannot be determined from an autopsy?

A Heavy Case of Typhoid

Henri Girard of Paris committed the perfect crime—almost.

The way J. H. H. Gaute and Robin Odell tell it in *The Murderers' Who's Who*, after blowing a family inheritance, Girard set out to locate another fortune. Charming Louis Pernotte into giving him power of attorney, Girard then insured Pernotte's life for 300,000 francs. Shortly thereafter, M. and Mme. Pernotte and their two children all came down with typhoid—a problem that couldn't, of course, have been related to the typhoid bacilli Girard had recently bought. Mme. Pernotte and the children survived; Pernotte died. Girard was heartbroken by his friend's death—but not too heartbroken to tell Mme. Pernotte that M. Pernotte owed him 200,000 francs!

Expanding his technique, Girard then tried poisonous mushrooms on his next two intended victims. They survived, but the one after that, a widow, succumbed a little too soon after her insurance purchase. The insurance companies investigated, La Sûreté became involved, and Girard sadly explained that he was unhappy and misunderstood despite his warm heart.

Perhaps wisely, he then swallowed one of his own doses before he could reach trial.

Other people have tried Girard's technique since then. Some have not succeeded. If any did, we don't know about them.

Secretors

First, because of genetic fingerprinting, it is possible to determine far more now than when I was in police work. Then, we could—about 60 percent of the time—determine blood type of the assailant from semen, spittle or other body fluids left on the victim's body.

That's because about 60 percent of the population are secretors, and about 40 percent are not.

A *secretor* is a person whose blood type can be determined from body fluids other than blood. A nonsecretor's blood type cannot be determined from any body fluid other than blood. The difference is probably genetically determined, but nobody knows why or how. After the gene-mapping project is complete, maybe we will know.

Police wish all sex criminals were secretors.

Now, with DNA fingerprinting, if the assailant has left any of his/her own body fluids behind, we may have enough to identify the assailant with almost certainty.

The Cause of Death

The pathologist can usually determine the cause of death, bearing in mind that almost always there is a chain of causes rather than a single cause. If you have ever seen a death certificate, you saw on it several lines that look like this:

Death was due to _____ ;
Due to _____ ;
Due to _____ ;
Due to _____ ;
Due to _____ ;
Due to _____ ;
Due to _____ ;
This is a legal recognition of a medical fact.

Legal Cause of Death

Under English common law, and under statute law in many states, death must occur within a year and a day following the injury to be considered murder. The reason for this originally was the medical uncertainty about cause of lingering death. It may well be *medically* true that the injury is still the cause of death, but in many jurisdictions it is no longer *legally* true. According to Black's — a very important legal reference source — the rule is obsolete, but the common-law presumption hasn't been overturned by statute in most jurisdictions.

In taking out an arrest warrant following a murder, the officer must be absolutely exact in what s/he says. In the past, courts have ruled arrests invalid and even overturned convictions because the warrant and the indictment based on the warrant did not state that the subject shot the victim *with a gun* (it could have been with a crossbow); drowned the victim *in water* (it could have been in a butt of Malmsey); or burned the victim *with fire* (it could have been with acid). This means that the findings of the examining pathologist are critical in making a case for murder. Consider these gray areas: If a person dies of a heart attack after the assailant sticks a gun in his face and threatens to shoot him, is that murder? (In most states, probably not.)

English common law, on which the statute law in all of the United States except Louisiana is based (Louisiana's law is based on the French Napoleonic Code), holds that any criminal is guilty of any result that a reasonable person would expect to follow the action the criminal took. That is, if the criminal takes a pistol and holds up a store and the pistol accidentally goes off and kills someone, then the criminal is guilty of murder, because any reasonable person would assume that a person who uses a loaded weapon in the commission of a felony intended murder. However, statute law varies from state to state, so before basing a story on this common law, you must check with your local district attorney, a lawyer, a law library, or the state attorney general's office. In Utah recently, a man who had shot and killed a pregnant woman, in front of her other children, was convicted of a lesser offense than capital murder because he insisted, and was able to convince a jury, that the loaded pistol he was holding to her head while robbing a video store "accidentally" went off.

Death by gun, knife, fire, bludgeoning—these are pretty obvious, and the autopsy is often little more than a legal formality. The serial killer who gets away with it for years not because nobody can find him but because nobody knows murder is happening is usually setting up apparent illnesses (typhoid fever), good accidents ("The Brides in the Bath"), doing careful strangulation ("The Death Angel"), or using poison. (How many do you want me to name?)

The brides in the bath: George J. Smith just couldn't seem to keep a wife.

He abandoned Beatrice Thornhill, his first wife and the only legal one. She didn't know until much later how lucky she was.

He was using the name Henry Williams when he "married"

Bessie Mundy. Poor Bessie died in her bathtub at Herne Bay, leaving a small fortune to her spouse.

The grieving widower next married Alice Burnham, who was possessed of small fortune. Ever provident, George saw to it she got life insurance. Poor Alice died in her bathtub in Blackpool. Her spouse, of course, collected.

His next wife, Margaret Elizabeth Lofty, also well insured, died in her bathtub in Highgate. This time more newspapers picked up the story, and when Mr. Burnham, Smith's previous father-in-law, heard the story, he was curious—very, very curious.

The police soon shared his curiosity.

Brilliant forensic pathologist Sir Bernard Spilsbury thought perhaps the murderer had "simultaneously lift[ed] the knees and press[ed] on the head, so that the body slid along the bath, taking the head under water" (Gaute and Odell 214). Because there was no sign of struggle whatever, and no marks except a slight bruise on the heel of one victim, police were not fully satisfied with that theory but were unable to come up with a better one. They decided to try an experiment. They enlisted the aid of a young woman who was an expert swimmer. Clad in a swimsuit, she sat down in a full bathtub, and a policeman standing at the end of the tub nearest her feet seized her by the heel and yanked. Instantly her feet flew up and the rest of her body slid down into the water. The woman, though alert, healthy and expecting the attack, nearly drowned. After she was revived, half an hour later, she said water was forced into her mouth and lungs so quickly she hadn't time to do anything, even hold her breath. (In early experiments, when police tried following Spilsbury's suggestion, she had plenty of time to resist.)

See Figure 8-1, which shows the sequence of the experiment.

The death angel: Poor Jeanne was so sweet. Even after her own children died one right after the other, she was still so happy to look after her nieces and nephews, and the children of her neighbors. In fact, she would beg for the opportunity; being around children made her feel closer to her dead darlings. When the babies died, as the poor things so often did, nobody was louder in grief at the funeral, in sympathy for the mother, than Jeanne. Nobody thought a thing—

Until a neighbor arrived home unexpectedly early and entered her baby's room, to catch Jeanne in the act of strangling the child.

Incredibly, Jeanne Weber was repeatedly caught in the act be-

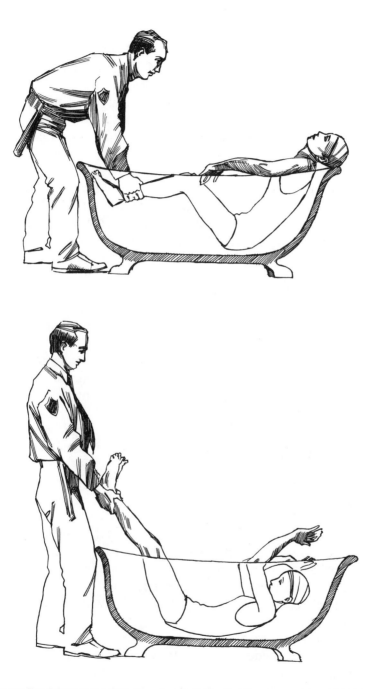

Figure 8-1. The Brides in the Bath Experiment. Notice that the shape of the old-fashioned tub certainly aided Smith in his scheme. Illustration by Tom Post.

fore doctors or police would pay any attention; police tended to ignore complaints from slums, and doctors kept insisting the babies had died of fits or convulsions or cramps. Even more incredibly, her neighbors and relatives allowed her to go on babysitting. She was tried once and acquitted; after that, she was hired to work in a children's home by a philanthropist who wanted to show how sorry society was about her being falsely accused! The children's home discharged her after several children were severely injured, but did not report her.

It was only after she had killed two more children that she was rearrested, this time winding up in a mental hospital rather than a prison. Two years later, she did the theoretically impossible: She succeeded in strangling herself to death.

Even after she died in 1910, some of the officials who had continued to insist on her innocence swore she had committed only one murder, the last one, in which the tiny victim was severely mutilated as well as manually strangled. Their explanation? She had been so often accused of murder that eventually her mind snapped and she did what she had been accused of!

Nobody was ever able to determine for sure whether Jeanne had killed her own children, though the evidence was strong, because decomposition had proceeded to the extent that the hyoid, cricoid and thyroid were no longer discernible.

Why did she do it? Nobody ever knew. Jeanne loved babies. She'd tell anybody so. And she played with them so nicely—as long as she was carefully watched every second.

Hidden Serial Killers

Why does this type of murder so often succeed? Why, even today, do we occasionally hear of investigation into a slightly suspicious death that leads to the discovery of a five, ten, twenty-year trail of corpses? It's not, generally, because medical science can't find the answer. It's because nobody ever suspected anything, and so no autopsy was ever performed.

Of course there are still tricky ones—like Carl Coppolino, whose wife died suddenly of a heart attack. He might have gotten away with it, if his rejected mistress (whose husband had also died of a convenient heart attack probably induced by the muscle relaxant Coppolino had provided her to inject into her husband) hadn't gone to the police after Carl married someone else only three weeks after his wife's death. When the rejected mistress tattled, Carmela Coppolino was exhumed. Not only was there evidence of some sort of injection — probably of the same muscle relaxant that had been used on the mistress's husband — but also of strangulation (her cricoid was crushed).

Figure 8-2 illustrates the relative location of the thyroid, the cricoid and the hyoid, which were also discussed in chapter seven.

Other cases of murder by injection include the killing on May 3, 1957, of Elizabeth Barlow, whose husband, Kenneth, under the guise of injecting an abortifacient to get rid of the six-week pregnancy she didn't want, instead repeatedly injected her with insulin until she died of induced acute hypoglycemia.

Proving Disguised Murder

This sort of thing tends to be extremely difficult to prove; indeed, any case involving exhumation is difficult to prove. There are several problems.

- First, after a body has been buried, it takes probable cause, not mere suspicion, to obtain a court order for exhumation. The family is likely to fight the order on the basis that their loved one's grave is being desecrated; if — as is most often the case — the suspect is a member of the family, it is difficult to distinguish between that sort of protest and the protest of the murderer.

- Second, embalming removes many of the evidences of crime. Remember that in embalming, as much as possible of the blood is drained from the body and replaced by embalming fluid.

- Third, the condition of the body despite embalming and a sealed coffin may not be good. In any climate but a constantly dry or freezing cold one, but especially in a hot, wet climate, the best embalming can do is delay decomposition for a short time. (That's one reason I strongly suspect that the body of Lenin on display in Russia is largely wax.) I once needed, for a novel, to know whether the body of a six-week-pregnant woman in Galveston, Texas, buried for three years, could be exhumed and the fetus's blood type determined. Pathologists in Galveston County assured me that not only could the fetus's

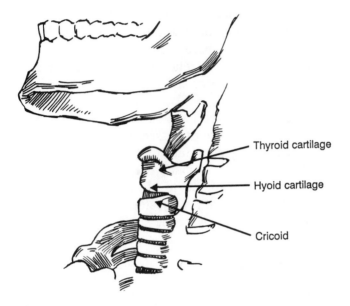

Thyroid cartilage

Hyoid cartilage

Cricoid

Figure 8-2. All of these are parts of the larynx, which contains many additional parts. Don't confuse the thyroid cartilage with the thyroid gland, which adjoins and attaches to it. Illustration by Tom Post.

blood type not be determined, it would almost certainly be impossible to determine even that the woman had been pregnant at the time of death. Scratch one intended plot complication.

- Fourth, even with minimal decay, some evidences are hard to locate. Can you imagine looking for a needle puncture in the body of a woman who has been dead for months? It's hard enough to find one in your own arm three hours after a flu shot.

- And finally, soil conditions can have considerable effect on the investigation. For example, in many areas, groundwater contains an appreciable quantity of arsenic. Although this arsenic fosters good preservation of the body, it also may make it impossible to determine whether the arsenic got into the body before or after death.

What if Some Body Parts Are Missing?

Another situation in which the pathologist may find it difficult if not impossible to determine the cause of death is that in which only part of the body has been located. But that, of course, depends on what the cause of death actually was. If the victim was shot in the head and the head was subsequently removed, there may be no obvious cause of death. In that case, assuming that a good suspect and probable cause for arrest are developed, the arrest warrant must state that X murdered Y on or about such-and-such a date in a manner that cannot be determined — the same type of statement that is necessary in a case such as that of L. Ewing Scott, whose victim's body was never found. In such a case, it is more difficult, but certainly not impossible, to get a conviction.

Tools of the Investigative Trade

What are some of the tools available in the forensic pathology laboratory? An uncopyrighted article by James Geer of the FBI's laboratory division mentions forensic serology, electrophoresis, liquid chromatography, gas chromatography, ion chromatography, mass spectrometry, "optical and instrumental methods of collecting, handling, preparing, identifying, and comparing hair, textile fibers, and other types of fibrous materials," atomic absorption analysis, "genetics, protein and enzyme chemistry, protein polymorphism . . . and isoelectric focusing and [its] application to bloodstain analysis" (91). Most large-town pathology laboratories have at least serology, liquid and gas chromatography, and mass spectrometry equipment handy; for things they do not possess, they may turn to the closest big-city laboratories, to state laboratories, or to the FBI laboratory. To find out what your town has available, talk with the coroner and/or medical examiner.

Let's get to some definitions now. *Serology* is the study of blood and other body fluids; *forensic serology*, of course, is the study of blood and body fluids in a criminal situation. *Electrophoresis* is a method of identifying chemicals by analyzing a small amount that has been burned. *Chromatography* and *spectrometry* are methods of identifying chemicals by using mixed chemical and computerized tests; the resultant colored bar graphs allow exact determination of chemicals present and their concentrations. We talked about atomic absorption analysis, also called neutron activation analysis, in reference to firearms evidence.

And what can scientists determine from all these tests? It's obvious, of course, that they can discover such things as what chemicals are present in or on the body and in what proportions. From stains left by the assailant on the victim, they may be able to determine sex and blood type of the assailant. If the victim yanked out some of the assailant's hair, very often scientists can determine the sex of the assailant from the hair (if it was not otherwise apparent).

By determining the trajectory of the knife or gun, the pathologist may determine the height of the assailant, the distance the assailant was from the victim, the handedness of the assailant. The trajectory is determined by the path the bullet or knife took through the clothing and through the body. But sometimes things get complicated in this area.

Unusual Problems

Hans Gross says that "it is possible to find large gun-shot wounds, while the dress covering them is not in the slightest degree injured." I would not believe this statement for a second, were it not for the case of Jack. (Remember the names are changed.)

This case occurred while I was still detective bureau secretary;

in fact, it was in the first few months, and the department had yet to learn that I am not unduly squeamish. Jack ran a small barbecue restaurant in a sleazy part of town. One evening, just about twilight, as he sat in his kitchen, listeners heard him involved in a loud quarrel. Then, quite suddenly, Jack got up and ran outside, apparently chasing the person he was quarreling with. Three shots were fired, and the next person to run outdoors found Jack on the ground dead, his pistol in his hand. His pistol had been fired twice. He had been killed by a shot from another pistol.

The body was hauled off to the emergency room, where detectives took custody of clothing before transferring the body to the morgue. The clothing was taken into the detective bureau. No crime lab yet existed in Albany, and the clothing was draped over chairs and a table in a witness room to allow the blood to dry. That was on Saturday.

On Monday, the chief of detectives went out in person to view the autopsy. About ten o'clock he called me from the morgue. There was a question about the trajectory of the fatal bullet, and he wanted me to go and examine the clothing. And here's where the whole thing got very, very complicated.

Jack had not been underdressed. He had on a bib apron, a button-up shirt, and a V-neck undershirt. The bullet had entered the left side of the chest at approximately the level of the nipple at a sharp angle, exiting on the right side below the rib cage (see Figure 8-3).

I examined the clothing carefully, and then I examined it again. There was not one trace of a bullet hole in any item of clothing. I went back to the phone and told Chief Summerford that. He told me I was too squeamish and sent me back to look again. I did, with the same results.

About ten minutes later, Chief Summerford, obviously furious, stormed in and searched the clothes himself—with the same results.

He decided maybe the bullet had parted the threads and gone through, allowing the cloth to close up once more. His wife, whose hobby was sewing, assured him that was impossible.

Because the trajectory of the bullet indicated that Jack had been shot by someone well above him as well as facing him, like maybe up in a tree, we looked at trees. There were some present, but there was no way whatever the person he chased out of his kitchen would have had time to climb one before the shots were fired.

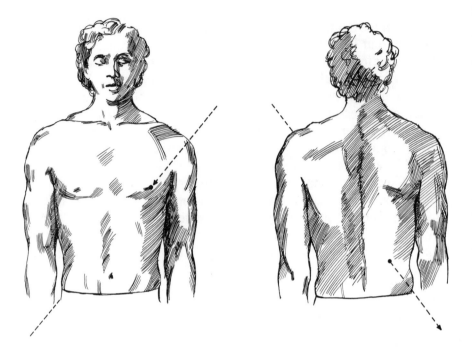

Figure 8-3. Trajectory of bullet from top to bottom and left to right. Illustration by Tom Post.

I thought maybe Jack had tripped over a tree root just as his assailant shot; so he would have been leaning or falling forward with his apron, shirt and undershirt falling away from his body so that the bullet entered above all of the clothing. Chief Summerford, wiser than I in the ways of men's clothing, said that was nonsense.

The case was never cleared. About six months after the shooting, the pistol that had fired the fatal shot was found in an abandoned house. The Bureau of Alcohol, Tobacco, and Firearms managed over the next couple of months to trace the gun through about twenty owners, the last two of whom had stolen it. The last one of those said the gun was stolen from him. There was known to be bad blood between him and Jack, and he was nervous, but there wasn't quite enough to make a case.

After talking with him for hours, one of the detectives invited me to see whether I could get anything out of him. I went back into the witness room and told him that the police knew he was lying. He insisted he wasn't, but it was obvious even to me that he was. I finally said, "Look, we've got about enough to make a case on you for murder. You're denying it, but you won't tell us what you were doing at the time. Whatever it was—even if it was illegal—it's a lot less serious than murder. So why don't you save us all a lot of trouble, and spill it?"

He said he'd tell me, but I told him he had to tell the detectives as well. He agreed, and the detectives came back in. What unfolded was a chilling tale indeed: He'd been stalking a woman, preparing to rob her. He described what she did, how she came back from shopping, went in her house, opened the draperies, as he watched from the shrubbery. Something happened to cause him to change his mind, and he left without committing the intended robbery.

Detectives located the woman, asked her what she had done that evening. She had a good memory or a good diary, I don't know which, but her horror as she confirmed everything he said she had done made it clear that he was watching her, not committing murder, the night Jack died.

Some of us continued to believe the suspect guilty, but after that alibi confirmation, we had no case. The suspect himself was murdered, in a poolroom brawl on Christmas Day a couple of years later.

And there the case rested.

By then I was to the point I didn't really care who shot Jack.

All I wished he would do was write me an anonymous letter and tell me *how* he did it.

By anybody's book, that one was impossible. If there was another thing anybody could have done to clear it, I don't know what it was.

But some of yesterday's "impossible" cases would now be very simple. Is this stain really blood? Is it really human blood? What blood type is it? Is it blood from the victim or the assailant? What chemicals are in this body that don't belong there? Are there enough of those chemicals present to be the cause of death?

The Murder of Napoleon

Arsenic and heavy metals do something particularly interesting: They get in the hair. This means that scientists can determine over how long a period this poison was administered, whether it was continuous or stopped and started, and—by means of determining who was always present when it was administered and who was never present when it was administered—determine who did it. There has been one fascinating and unexpected side effect of this research.

For generations, the official dogma has been that Napoleon Bonaparte died of cancer while in English custody on the Island of St. Helena. For generations, many French historians have insisted that the Emperor Napoleon I was poisoned. It is now certain that the French were right. Napoleon Bonaparte died of arsenic poisoning. The brilliant investigative work that led to that conclusion—which included such feats as tracking down and analyzing hair cuttings taken from the body by grieving servants and passed down as family heirlooms—have even implicated a suspect.

I am not a forensic chemist, and in general I do not know how these things work. Even when I have watched the tests given I did not understand what I was watching. But that was all right. What was important to know was not how the tests work but that they do indeed work, so that I would know what to ask for.

Murder or Suicide?

But sometimes nobody can know what to ask for: Sometimes the truth is so bizarre that even after the autopsy and all the detective work have combined to produce it, it remains unbelievable. Such was the case of Mike.

Mike was found dead about two o'clock in the morning near his car, which had plunged off the shoulder of the road, gone into a ditch, and lodged against an embankment so that the passenger's door of the two-door sedan could not be opened. But Mike hadn't died in the wreck. No, he'd died from a single blast from the snake gun—a short, small-gauge shotgun—that lay between him and the car (see Figure 8-4).

We could see where the car had paused on the side of the road, had probably sat there for a while. We could tell that the snake gun had been fired inside the car, that it had hit Mike on the upper-right forehead. We surmised that Mike had paused there with his foot on the brake, without taking the car out of gear, while he and his passenger quarreled; that the passenger shot Mike with the snake gun; that Mike's foot then slipped off the brake and onto the accelerator, causing the car to drive off the shoulder. The passenger, finding himself unable to open his own door, pushed Mike's body out of the way and crawled out, leaving the bloody palm print of his right hand on the driver's door where he had braced himself climbing out.

That left two unanswered questions: Why had the snake gun been tossed outside the car? (We'd expect the suspect to leave it in the car or take it with him.) And why had Mike's body wound up where it did? (That was farther than it had to be moved.)

But if the car wreck had left the suspect a little dazed, both of those questions were at least semianswerable.

Never mind the rest of the night—the lying braggart hearing police at a coffee shop talking about the case, running his own mouth at the bus stop, and sending Johnny Patton, Bob Prickett and me on an all-night chase across three counties. Never mind the next six weeks, while detectives chased down everything they could find and I compared that bloody palm print to the palm print of every known acquaintance of Mike.

And then one night, when I was working 6:00 P.M. to 2:00 A.M. and things were quiet, I decided to search the palm print the same way I would search a fingerprint. So what if the FBI said a nonsuspect ident from a palm print was impossible? It certainly would be from their huge files, but we probably didn't have much more than 700 palm prints, and this was a good, clear one containing two good deltas to work from.

So I started searching—and after about four nights of work, I

Figure 8-4. Relative positions of automobile, victim and snake gun. Illustration by Tom Post.

found the matching print. Only then did I look at the name — and nearly went into shock. I was looking at Mike's own palm print.

But the palm print on the door could not have been made by a body being dragged out. It could only have been made by someone leaning against the door while getting out of the car.

I could hardly wait for the next morning, to call the medical examiner and start asking questions. "Based on your examination, do you think Mike could have lived any period of time after being shot?"

"He probably lived about half an hour."

"Could he have been conscious and capable of volitional action at any time during that half an hour?"

"He might have been conscious and able to move around for about five to seven minutes."

My opinion of the case changed abruptly. Here was my new scenario: Mike had stopped his car up on the roadside, wrestling with his suicide decision, and then shot himself. His foot slipped off the brake onto the gas, and the car plunged down the embankment. Dazed, Mike staggered out of the car, leaning heavily against the door, and then reached in to get the snake gun, perhaps to use it as a crutch. He dropped it, took a few more steps, staggered, and fell full length. That would account for everything.

Mine was a minority view — a minority of one.

Until a few days later, when Mike's girlfriend — we must assume she was less than the world's greatest housekeeper — showed up at the detective bureau, bringing Johnny Patton a note from Mike she had just found — six weeks late — on the mantel. It was a nobody-loves-me / everybody-hates-me / I'm-going-out-in-the-garden-to-eat-some-worms kind of note. It could have been interpreted as a suicide note; it could have been interpreted as something else. But added to what we already had —

I was still a minority, but no longer a minority of one. I believe, though, that the case is still carried as an unsolved murder.

Knowing what to ask for. Knowing how to interpret what you get. That was important to the investigator's role in the autopsy when Gross was writing his first criminology text, and that's what's important today — not that the investigator know how the tests work, but that the investigator know what to ask for.

And what can, and what cannot, be done.

That's important for the writer, too.

TABLE 8
The Person Who Finds the Body

Some writers, such as P.D. James and Dorothy Sayers, like to spend a good bit of time examining the reactions of the first person— usually uninvolved and innocent—who finds the body. What will such a person notice? Think about ways you can use these facts to create red herrings.

- If there is blood and gashing, an unexpecting (and unsuspecting) discoverer of the body will rarely see past those injuries. S/he will not, later, be able to describe clothing, hair, eyes and so forth.

- If the victim was strangled, the discoverer will notice if the body is hanging but may not otherwise notice anything around the neck, as his/her attention will be focused on the protruding tongue, bulging eyes, swollen and suffused face, and froth (often bloody) around the mouth. If a male strangulation victim is naked, the discoverer may notice the erect or semi-erect penis. Again, clothing, coloring, and so forth almost certainly will go unnoticed.

- Even in natural death, there may be a deceptive appearance of violence which will be very distressing to the finder. In some cases, the victim of a heart attack may bite his tongue, bleed from the mouth and nose, and dash about knocking things over, presenting the exact appearance of a violent struggle. In other cases, the heart attack victim will die instantly; I have seen such victims found hours after death still sitting on the toilet or leaning over the fence of a dog kennel.

- If the victim has been dead several days, the first thing noticeable is the odor. I have heard it described as sickly sweetish, but it doesn't seem sweetish to me. I find it horrible and indescribable. It is like nothing else including animal carrion, and it cannot be mistaken for anything else even by a person who has never smelled it before. Even a fresh corpse, dead of violence, has a smell that seems to be comprised of stale raw meat, stale blood, and combined feces and urine, as the sphincters normally relax in death and release feces and urine.

- The corpse dead several days, unless it has been kept extremely cold, will have begun to rot. The entire body will be swollen with the bruise-like colors of decay. A bluish film may cover the open eyes, making even dark eyes appear blue. By this time, body fluids have soaked clothing, making it harder to observe so that even a normally good observer may not be able to distinguish color of anything but the victim's hair.

- A body that has spent some time in cold, but not freezing, flowing water may be mistaken for a fresh body, but the epidermis—the top layer of skin, with all its hairs, suntan, calluses, scars and other marks—will have sloughed off, leaving behind the dermis, which will appear like the skin of a delicate and very young person never exposed to sun or work. The nails, slipping off with the epidermis, will leave behind delicate glistening pinkish nail beds, which may look like short but well-tended nails. Thus the body of a French peasant woman in her twenties was once, several hundred years ago, mistaken for the body of a noblewoman of fifteen. Before the error was discovered, a frantic search had taken place for the source of the found body and the body of the missing woman, and two men were near execution for a nonexistent murder.

- In real life, the discoverer of the body may well be the murderer, drawn back by his/her own nervousness about the situation, or s/he may be a perfectly innocent intruder on the crime scene. The nervous murderer at this point may appear as distraught as if s/he were totally innocent.

- Discovering a body, like being a crime victim, is extremely stressful and may lead to Posttraumatic Stress Disorder. As a result of this nervous condition, the finder's memories of the scene may become extremely vague, disorganized and unreliable. Apparent falsehoods told by the finder are at least as likely to be the result of shock as the result of deliberate attempts to mislead.

INSIDE THE CRIME LAB

The zealous Investigating Officer will note on his walks the footprints found on the dust of the highway; he will observe the tracks of animals, of the wheels of carriages, the marks of pressure on the grass where someone has sat or lain down, or perhaps deposited a burden. He will examine little pieces of paper that have been thrown away, marks or injuries on trees, displaced stones, broken glass or pottery . . . .
                                          —Hans Gross,
                                          Criminal Investigation

I've discussed what the investigator may find at the crime scene and how s/he should package the things found there. But what happens to those items once they reach the lab? And more important, what can the lab discover that can help the detective?

Let's look now not at how the lab does the work, which would need a whole library of books the size of this one, but rather at what the lab can determine from working with those bits of evidence.

Bombings

If you followed the story of the airplane that exploded over Locherbie, Scotland, you are undoubtedly aware that one of the most significant bits of evidence was a fragment, no larger than a fingernail, of a detonating device. Crime laboratories often are able to make significant findings from fragments of evidence that small. The task is not easy, however, and if the crime-scene investigator doesn't know what to collect, or how to package it, or what to tell and ask the lab, these findings may be impossible.

Dynamite

Dynamite does not usually contain any kind of tracer that would allow it, after it is detonated, to be tracked to its source.

Dry dynamite is reasonably safe. It is not likely to be detonated accidentally; it needs some sort of "cap" or detonating device. You've seen on television people detonating dynamite by firing a gun at it. It's possible, but not easy enough to be practical.

Wet dynamite is another matter, especially if it's been wet very long. It begins to separate into its component parts, until by the time it has developed a greasy yellowish or off-white look, it becomes as unstable as pure nitroglycerine—which means that a knock can set it off.

Laboratory Findings in Bombings

- It is usually possible to determine what type of explosive was used. Because many explosive manufacturers deliberately include a *chemical signature*—certain inert but easily identifiable chemicals that vary slightly from batch to batch—it is often possible to determine the source in detail, by finding out first what manufacturer made that batch of explosives and when that batch was made, and then tracing that batch to its purchaser. All too often, however, the trail hits a dead end; either somebody has lost track of the materiel (frequently, this means it was sold to somebody nobody wants to admit selling explosives to) or it has been stolen.

- It is frequently possible to determine precisely where the explosion took place. In a building, that may mean little, but in an airplane, for example, it may be possible to find out in whose baggage the bomb was placed. That would be a major lead as to who might be responsible for the bombing.

- It is often possible to determine what the triggering device was, and to trace the device back to its manufacturer and then forward to its purchaser. In the Mark Hofmann bombings in Utah, much of the equipment and supplies used to manufacture the triggering device had been purchased quite openly from Radio Shack, which of course intended it for quite different uses.

The Mormon Forgery Bomber

Who was Mark Hofmann?

In October 1985, a bomb disguised as a just-delivered package exploded in a downtown Salt Lake City office building, killing a businessman. Later the same day, a second bomb which had been left near the patio of another businessman detonated when the intended victim's wife picked up the package. For several days, associates of the two men were rushed into hiding by authorities fearing for their safety and absolutely baffled as to motive; although the two men had been involved in a financial scheme that had gone belly-up, it seemed unlikely that anybody would want to use bombs as a means of revenge. Then, on a hill outside LDS (Mormon) Church-owned Deseret Gym, a third bomb exploded when Mark Hofmann was getting into his car. Unlike the other two victims, Hofmann—who had been involved with the businessmen in other ways, but not in the financial scheme—survived.

At first, Hofmann was thought to be another innocent victim, and authorities began to look elsewhere than the ill-fated financial scheme for motives, but within days after the third bombing, the trail led back to Hofmann himself. A workshop inside his house proved to be the location where the bombs were built, and sales people in a nearby Radio Shack store remembered selling him some of the items that later became parts of the bombs. Speculation was rife as to where Hofmann had been returning from when his car exploded, and whether the third bomb had been intended for another person or an attempt at suicide. Although Hofmann eventually confessed and in January 1987 pled guilty, many of these questions were never resolved.

However, investigation unraveled an incredibly tangled web of forgery, fraud, swindling and murder. Over many years beginning while he was still in college, Hofmann—among other things, a rare-document dealer—had "discovered" many rare and valuable documents from American history and specifically from LDS (Mormon) history. After the bombings, many of the documents

were revealed as forgeries, and many others — possibly legitimate — remained highly suspect. But Hofmann had finally over-
reached himself by "finding" a collection that seemingly did not
exist, and then selling the collection — sight unseen — to one person while mortgaging it to another. Attempting to cover up the
fraud, he began methodically murdering his victims. Nobody was
ever able to determine who the third bomb was intended for, and
Hofmann refused to tell.

Several books have been published on the case; unfortunately, most of them are more or less hostile to the LDS (Mormon) Church, which more reasonably should be considered another victim of Hofmann's fraud.

A joke circulating in Utah at the time went like this:
Joker: Hey, have you heard, Mark Hofmann was pardoned?
Victim: You're kidding! How in the world —
Joker (grinning): Yeah, the pardon was signed by Brigham
Young.

Laboratory Determination From Small Evidence

Let's go on, now, to look at what the lab can determine from other
things. A good place to start is with bloodstains. One of the major
pieces of evidence in the Sam Sheppard case, discussed earlier, was
the pillowcase Marilyn Sheppard's head had been lying on. Among
the many bloodstains on it, there was a distorted but somewhat
symmetrical one which could, given sufficient exercise of the imagination, appear to be the place where a tool was laid, the pillow
folded over it, and the tool later removed. The prosecution maintained that the mark was that of some never-named surgical instru-
ment, which Sheppard used to bludgeon Marilyn; the defense contended — uselessly, in the original trial, though it was an important
element in later appeals — that the mark was actually made when
the bloody pillowcase was crumpled over on itself.

Bloodstain Evidence

Blood can reveal many things. It can reveal species: Is this
blood on the suspect's clothing human blood or — as he claims — dog

blood from when he took his injured pet to the veterinarian? Blood type—can this be the blood of the victim or the suspect, or is it that of someone else? It is important to remember that in all cases, the older the blood is, the less information will be obtainable from it. In blood more than a year old, it may not be possible to obtain much more than the species and the ABO type; the DNA fingerprint may persist for years, but the older the blood, the less likely that any test results will be reliable.

Of course, the investigator and the laboratory will at times be looking for different information from blood found at the scene of the crime and from blood found later on the person, clothing, vehicle, or other possessions of the suspect.

Obviously if the blood at the scene is that of the assailant and, as usual, the crime is discovered promptly, with reasonable luck the blood type and the DNA fingerprint of the assailant can be obtained. But even if the blood belongs to the victim, there are many things it can reveal about the suspect and about the manner in which the crime occurred. Quite a lot of research has centered on this matter, and a terrific recent book is *Interpretation of Bloodstain Evidence at Crime Scenes*, by William G. Eckert and Stuart James. It is part of the Elsevier Series in Practical Aspects of Criminal and Forensic Investigations; although it's the only one of the series I've needed to consult, the entire series (listed inside the front endpapers of the book) looks splendid for a crime writer's personal library as well as for an evidence technician's library. Of course, they should all be available through interlibrary loan.

Although all aspects of bloodstains are important, Dr. Paul Kirk, who wrote a pioneering book on blood at the crime scene, contends that "No other type of investigation of blood will yield so much useful information as an analysis of the blood distribution patterns" (Eckert and James 11-12). Kirk, who was involved with the Sheppard appeals, testified in 1955 that he

> was able to establish the relative position of the attacker and victim at the time of the . . . beating. He was able to determine that the attacker administered blows with a left hand, which was significant in that Dr. Sheppard was right-handed.
>
> (Eckert and James 12)

As a result of his testimony, interest in bloodstain evidence—which had been substantial throughout the history of criminal investigation — grew considerably, and forensic scientists as well as investigating officers realized even more the need for careful studies of the characteristics of blood in various situations. Up to that time, each individual investigator, working on his or her own, would decide what the bloodstains appeared to indicate, sometimes on the basis of experiments with beef or chicken blood (which does not have exactly the same characteristics as human blood) and sometimes on the basis of sheer guesswork. Working under a government grant, H.L. MacDonnell did several painstaking studies, which were published in 1971 and 1973. By 1983, the International Association of Bloodstain Pattern Analysts had been organized, and the study continues. Eckert and James suggest that careful study of bloodstains can provide the following types of information:

- Source of the blood — human or animal? Which human or animal?
- Relative positions of persons and objects in the area at the time of the attack.
- Distances the blood flew, and speed.
- Whether impact was from sharp or blunt object.
- Number of impacts.
- Elapsed time between impact and study.
- Movements of persons and objects after the attack.

By providing this information, the study can help to determine which possible witnesses are telling the truth; can provide additional means of judging time of death; and can help to sort out findings from other investigative and laboratory work.

For a more precise discussion of bloodstains, see the entire Eckert and James book, particularly the section beginning on page thirteen.

But in order for any of these desirable results to occur, the investigator at the scene has the primary responsibility for — what? For seeing to it that s/he fulfills the duties that are always the primary responsibility of the investigator on the scene: making careful notes; making careful photographs (preferably color, preferably with a measuring device included in every photograph); and taking careful, triangulated measurements. The investigator must *always* remember that no color film is fully dependable for showing subtle gradations in color, so notes are critical; furthermore, photographs not done very carefully may distort the truth. (We've all seen photos in which someone's feet, placed in the foreground, appear ten times their real size.)

Cameras and Film

At the time that I entered police work, the Albany Police Department was still using a Speed Graphic. That's the camera you see reporters and police photographers using in old movies—the one that's so tough that reporters could knock somebody in the head with it and then go on taking pictures. When Chief Summerford first instructed me to learn to use it, I was intimidated by the very sight of that camera.

Once you learn how to use it, however, there's practically nothing you can do to mess up pictures on it; it's far less fussy than many cameras. The huge (four-by-five-inch) negative allows enlargements for courtroom use with practically no grain, whereas a 35mm negative enlarged to eleven-by-sixteen is almost always going to look somewhat grainy. Its film packs and sheet films also prevent waste: If I use only four shots on a roll of film and need the pictures this afternoon, the other shots are wasted; if I use only four shots on a film pack, I can pull those four out and develop them and still have the other twelve shots left. And in a small darkroom, sheet film is far easier to work with blind than roll film.

But for all practical purposes, the day of the Speed Graphic is gone. Even black-and-white film for it now costs a small fortune, and I doubt color film is even available except through incredibly expensive special orders. Most police photography now is done almost entirely in color with 35mm cameras and film.

What kind of color film? A good photographer—or a writer intending to play tricks with photography in fiction—will take the time to read all available information on all films and determine which is the best to use now. Nobody can possibly say which is going to be best forever, because manufacturers are constantly improving film and processes.

In general, most crime-scene photographers use whatever camera the department supplies, and keep a personal camera and more departmental film in their car so that if they get a call in the middle of the night, they can go straight to the scene without having to detour by the police station.

It is important to remember that photography, when produced incompetently or with intent to mislead, particularly in a blood-spatter situation, can cause serious problems.

In general, police photography does not use filters of any kind. It is important to be able to swear, in court, that what the photograph shows is as nearly as possible *exactly* what the photographer saw. But most photographers know a few tricks. One is that if you shoot black-and-white panchromatic film through a filter the same color as your subject, that color seems considerably lighter in the picture; if you shoot through a complementary color filter, the color in the scene seems considerably darker. Thus, by using a red filter, you could effectively do away with a lot of the blood in the scene; by using a green filter, you could darken the blood.

In crime-scene investigations, it just doesn't happen. But in fiction? Ah, in fiction . . . what can *you* do with the possibilities?

But read a good camera book before you start on those possibilities. In this area, errors can make you look stupid.

Type of Blood-Spatter Patterns

The type of spatter pattern is determined by several factors, including the force with which the blood falls (is it dripping from a vein, spurting from an artery, slung from a weapon raised to make another blow, oozing from a dying victim?), the distance it falls, the type of surface it lands on, and whether it lands vertically or at an angle. If all these factors are considered, it is possible to trace the blood back to its converging point, just as one would do by extending the point a bullet impacted back through a hole in the wall where it penetrated, to determine where it was fired.

Some of these things have been reduced now to a formula — not one simple enough to do by hand, but one which can be put on any computer that can work with Basic. This program is included in the appendix to the Eckert and James book.

Eckert and James, and all other blood pattern investigators, warn against trying to make the blood reveal too much. Insufficient evidence is insufficient evidence, no matter what it consists of, and overinterpretation of insufficient evidence can lead to serious errors. (That's a terrific idea for use in fiction.)

Fingerprints, toolmarks, footprints, fabric imprints, and so forth can be made in blood, as well as in any other substance. In such a situation, the pattern must be carefully studied, as well as anything the blood itself reveals. That is, careful measurements and photographs are essential, and the item carrying the print, if possible, must be sent to the laboratory.

We've already talked a lot about fingerprints. Let's go on now and see what can be determined about some other items.

Tiremarks

From tire tracks, it is possible to determine the size of the vehicle, how heavily it is loaded, and the make of the tire. Each year, manufacturers make available to police agencies photographs of their new products, and data bases of this information are available to forensic scientists. If any tire manufacturer fails to cooperate, it is always possible to buy a tire of the type in question and make a data base entry.

When a suspect tiremark is first photographed and then cast in plaster of Paris, it is thereafter treated by the lab exactly as if it were a footprint.

Because each tire on each vehicle wears individually, if the suspect vehicle is located fairly soon — within a few hundred miles or so, and before the tire is changed — it is possible to say that this particular tire track was made by this particular tire and — usually — on this particular vehicle.

Tools and Toolmarks

What are toolmarks? They are the marks — most often various types of striations, or ridged, linear markings — made by any object other than the weapon used in the commission of a crime. If at all possible, the toolmark itself — the doorframe that carries the marks of the prybar, the safe and safe door which have been opened — should be transported to the laboratory. If this is completely impossible, then dental molding should be used to create an exact impression of the mark. Great care must be exercised to prevent distortion.

At the laboratory, technicians using comparison microscopes can almost always determine whether this mark was made by this suspect tool. If the suspect tool is not available, the lab can provide some information that will help investigators look for the tool; however, the likelihood of their being able to provide exact descriptions, brand names, and so forth is fairly small.

If you are curious as to how this would work, take a piece of lightweight but fairly wide metal of some sort and twist it in two. Then, using a magnifying glass, examine the ends where the metal parted. What you are looking at, in vastly simplified form, is what the lab will work with.

Footprints

If you've read Arthur Upfield's Australian mysteries, you've read a lot about tracking, trackers, what they can determine from footprints. I've never met anybody who could tell as much about footprints as Upfield's half-Abo detective, but I'm not saying it's impossible. Some people may be able to tell that much.

If you've read P.D. James's *Devices and Desires*, you've come across a more recent—and a more reasonable in terms of what is generally possible—use of footprints. In that case, because the Bumble brand sneakers with their bee on the sole were brand new, the brand and size were all anyone could determine. Generally, if the print is good and the shoes are distinctive, as sneakers usually are, the size and brand can be determined. How does this work? Every year, or with every design change, shoe manufacturers submit to law-enforcement laboratories information on the patterns on the sneaker soles. If—as may happen—some manufacturers decline or neglect to submit these patterns, the examiners simply purchase a pair of the sneakers in question. So books or computerized data banks of the patterns on distinctive shoe soles—available only to laboratory technicians, not to the general public—are constantly kept up to date, the same way data banks of tiremarks are kept current.

But no matter how smooth and nondistinctive the soles began, the shoes begin to differ as they begin to wear. The more they wear, the more different they become; by the time they have had fairly heavy wear, a good forensic scientist given the photograph or cast of the print and the shoe that made it, can say with absolute certainty that this shoe made this footprint. (Of course, that does not necessarily mean that the suspect was wearing the shoe, so that's always something writers can play with.)

The patterns of bare feet, generally, don't tell much except the size of the feet. But in a few rare instances, the footprint pattern—

which, like fingerprints and palm prints, consists of friction ridges — can be determined. In those cases, once a suspect is developed, an identification can be made as easily as by fingerprints.

I missed my one chance to make a footprint identification, when a barefoot burglar walked on top of furniture in a furniture store. He left perfectly good fingerprints another place, and he was too grotty for me to want to footprint him. I've kind of regretted missing the opportunity, but every time I think of his feet and his state of health ("I gots the syphs," he told me), I remember why I stuck with the fingerprints.

Fabric Impressions

The burglar had crawled through the kitchen exhaust fan into the restaurant, picking up an enormous quantity of grease on the way. Once in, he sat down briefly on an unopened crate of paper towels, leaving a perfect impression of the seat of his denim jeans. Shortly thereafter, a suspect was developed by other means. Doc and I couldn't make a positive identification of the grease print of his rear end, but we were sure enough to send the suspect jeans and the top of the crate to the laboratory for examination, and shortly thereafter the laboratory was sure enough to make the jury sure enough to get a conviction.

That's only one use of fabric impressions. As unlikely as it might sound, the intense impact of an automobile hitting a person may be sufficient to leave an impression of the person's clothing on the bumper; or blood may instantaneously splash out, soak the clothing, and leave an impression in blood of the clothing on the bumper. (Of course, in that case, the victim's blood alone may be enough for an identification, but on the other hand, it may not.)

Forensic Geology

Remember the scene in a Sherlock Holmes story where Holmes, observing the mud stains on Watson's trousers and shoes, tells Watson all the places he has been that day? Normally, in a small area — small in this case including the average city — there won't be quite that many different types of soil; certainly there won't be that many that can be distinguished by the naked eye. (And yet, when I was working as a state-sponsored amateur on an archaeological dig that was carbon-14 dated to more than 1,300 years ago and that covered less than 2,000 square feet, we had four different and highly distinctive soils, including sand, red clay, loam, and a yellow clay that apparently had been hauled a considerable distance and used to make a pavement. Certainly anybody could distinguish the shoes of a person who had been on that dig from those of one who had not.) At the very least, forensic geologists can usually determine whether the soil from this shoe or this tire *could* have come from a suspect location; when that determination is combined with what might have been learned from the shoe prints or the tire tracks at that location, the likelihood that this suspect is indeed the perp increases considerably.

In some cases, such as the situation of a rare, imported soil, the possibilities increase geometrically. In George Chesbro's *Second Horseman Out of Eden*, a letter from an abused child to Santa mailed in New York contains small amounts of a type of soil found only in the Amazon rain forest. Once the soil's source is determined, Mongo and his long-suffering brother are off on a crusade to discover how the envelope wound up in New York and where the child is located.

In real life, the results aren't usually quite that dramatic. But the possibilities are always there, and many are the times that I have used the evidence vacuum to collect microscopic evidence from the floorboard of a suspect vehicle to send it, with samples of soil from the area where the crime occurred, to the laboratory; many are the times the reports have come back telling me that the soil found in the floorboard of the car, presumably deposited there from the shoes of the suspect, could have come from the sample area. "Could have" is usually about the best the scientists can do, so this type of evidence normally must be combined with other evidence.

Fireclay

Fireclay combines the work of the forensic geologist with the work of the forensic paleontologist. So first—what is fireclay?

It is the insulating substance packed in the walls of a safe to protect the contents from fire and heat as long as possible. Fireclay is composed of sand, fine clay, and other minerals, and it almost always includes diatomaceous earth—earth that was once at the bottom of the sea. It contains fossil remnants of many microscopic sea creatures, and microscopic examination can almost always determine whether the fireclay on the suspect's shoes, in his trouser cuffs, and rubbed into his gloves is from the same source as the fireclay in the safe lining.

Safecrackers!

Like bank robbers and forgers, safecrackers used to be the cream of the crop of criminals. Now amateurs have taken over all three fields.

Despite the tales about safecrackers who used sandpaper on their fingers and then could feel when the tumblers dropped, so that they could open the safe using the dial, such safecrackers are extremely rare. Most often safes are peeled, burned or blown.

A *blown* safe has had holes drilled into it and explosives inserted into the holes. When the explosives are detonated, theoretically the safe blows open. More often the safe's contents are destroyed as well. Really good safecrackers don't blow safes.

A *burned* safe is opened when the part surrounding the dial is destroyed by an oxyacetylene blowtorch and the dial is removed; a similar technique can be used to remove the trunk's lock and retrieve lost trunk keys to your car. Some safecrackers cut all the way around the door.

A *peeled* safe is a professional job. The first time you see a peeled safe, you can scarcely believe your eyes. It looks like a sardine can cut open with an old-style blade can opener by a person on a fishing trip—except that the "blade" was a prybar and the "sardine can" may have three layers of walls including two inches or more of metal and six inches or more of fireclay.

Forensic Botany

Forensic botany sounds unlikely. What does the study of plants—other than marijuana and opium poppies—have to do with crime?

A whole lot. Like forensic geology, forensic botany can help to determine who has been where.

Pollen, leaves and flowers are all useful. In the landmark 1960 Australian kidnapping of Graeme Thorne, the victim's body was found six weeks later, wrapped in a rug tied into a bundle.

Scientists were able to determine from fungus spores found on the boy's shoes that he was murdered within hours of his abduction.

(The spores would have required six weeks to reach maturity.) But far more important, they found many fragments of a pinkish mortar and building stone, and among the large quantity of plant matter found in or on the bundle were large (by laboratory standards) quantities of debris from two different types of cypress tree. One was common, but the other was extremely rare — so rare that when they finally found a house that was built of the pink stone and had both of the cypress trees in its yard, and when they then learned that the previous occupant of the house, a man who had moved away on the very day of the kidnapping, had already been considered a suspect for other reasons, they were sure they had the perp.

And indeed they did. Stephen Leslie Bradley confessed and then retracted the confession, but the evidence was overwhelming. He was convicted and sentenced to life in prison.

Not all forensic botany is that impressive, and it can rarely stand alone. But when it is put together with the results of forensic geology, it can be extremely useful both as an investigative tool and as a court exhibit.

Hair

Human hair is somewhat problematical. Time after time, brilliant laboratory work has invented a method of positively establishing that this hair came from this body, and time after time, the method has been proven unreliable. DNA fingerprinting may help, but even it may be less positive than one would wish, quite simply because hair itself is dead. Only the hair bulb — the hair root — itself can be positively "fingerprinted," and even then only if it is at least halfway fresh — that is, before the bulb has either totally dried out or begun to rot. Hair evidence rarely includes the bulb, unless it was pulled out by the roots, as does sometimes happen in a violent crime.

However, hair evidence can be used to rule out many things. Species can almost always be determined, and it is usually possible to distinguish head hair from pubic hair. Race can frequently be determined from hair, and certainly it is commonly possible to determine that this particular hair did *not* come from this particular head.

But in general, the best positive identification that can be made right now is that this hair *could* have come from this person.

You will, by the way, find older books written while a method now obsolete was in use, that insist that this or that method is certain. At the time that this book is being written — the very beginning of 1992—there is no definite method of determining which hair came from whom, unless the root bulb is intact.

Sorry.

Check with the FBI next year. The situation is likely to change.

Fibers

Fibers, like hairs, botanic evidence and geological evidence, are somewhat circumstantial. The laboratory can determine quite a lot, including composition, origin (animal—wool or mohair? Plant—cotton or linen? Synthetic—nylon or orlon?), color, and often even dye lot, but it usually cannot say positively that this fiber came from this carpet or article of clothing and no other.

Even so, quite a lot of information can be derived. When the Shroud of Turin was subjected to intensive examination, much of the work was somewhat similar to that which might be done on crime-scene materials. A basic tenet of criminalistics is that when two items come in contact—whether the items are automobiles or human beings—there will be exchange of microscopic particles. (This is part of the reason for the very careful examination of the person and clothing of both victims and suspects.) This tenet was applied to the Shroud, because the assumption was that if it had been in Palestine 2,000 years ago, despite its history since then some pollen and so forth from that area and that time should still be clinging to it. Such pollens and dust particles indeed were found, and no trace of pigments that would have been used in painting were located. But other, less explicable, materials were present. Among the numerous submicroscopic pieces of fiber clinging to it were some pink fibers from a synthetic material that had never been used for anything other than women's girdles. Investigators confessed themselves baffled by that one. The only reasonable explanation was that an earlier investigator or photographer had come into contact with such a girdle, carried off fibers from it on his clothing, and later rubbed some of those fibers onto the Shroud.

Paint and Varnish

There are three situations in which these are likely to be useful. The first is when a victim has been assaulted or murdered in one location and then moved to another. In that case, the presence of paint or varnish (or any other chemical substance, such as motor oil or printer's ink) on the clothing or body may lead back to the location where the attack occurred, which in turn may lead to a suspect who had access to that spot.

The second situation occurs when the paint or varnish dust is in the air of the known crime scene, and this dust can be sought on the clothing of the suspect.

The third — and most common — use for paint occurs in a hit-and-run or an automobile murder. Very often paint chips off, and although these paint chips may convey nothing but color to the layman, they convey far more to the laboratory technician. Ford's blue car and Cadillac's blue car and Toyota's blue car are not the same blue. They contain slight or great color differences, and great differences in composition, layering, and so forth: An expensive automobile may have many layers of paint baked on, a cheap automobile may have no more than three or four layers. Of course, if a car has been repainted, either professionally or by a teenager with a paint brush and a left-over half-bucket of house paint, these facts also may be determined by the layers of paint. Next time you or a neighbor has a minor fender bender, have a look at some of the paint chips before the fender is fixed, and see what you can tell just with a small magnifying glass.

Glass

Glass is another circumstantial material. But it can prove a lot.

Scientists maintain files of the color, chemical composition and fractile characteristics of automobile headlight glass, so that a fragment found at the scene of a hit-and-run will help to determine within a few possibles the make and model of an automobile. When that information is combined with the paint chips often found with the glass, the color of the vehicle also becomes available.

Given several pieces of glass, scientists can determine from which side of the glass the impact came, whether it was a blunt impact or a sharp impact, and sometimes the force of the blow.

If the investigating officer or technician has made the usual careful records, it is almost always possible to determine whether glass was broken from the inside or the outside, even if an "inside job" was covered up by breaking glass and then putting the fragments inside to make it appear that the glass was broken from the outside.

Documents

Document examination presents some odd problems, and I'm not 100 percent sure it even belongs in a book that is primarily devoted to crime-scene work and subsequent laboratory work. It's another topic that would take several books this size to cover completely, and it is one of the few fields in which, in some ways, we are regressing rather than progressing. But there are reasons for the problems.

Handwriting

Please don't confuse handwriting identification with handwriting analysis. Handwriting identification is a science; handwriting analysis is considered by many people to be a pseudoscience. Handwriting identification attempts to decide who did, or sometimes who did not, write a particular document; handwriting analysis attempts to discern the personality traits of the person who did the writing.

Handwriting identification looks at many factors, some of them conscious but many of them so habitual they are totally beyond conscious control. These include the slant of the letters, the way the letters are joined or separated, the use of capitals in place of small letters and vice versa, the shapes of individual letters, the shapes of buckles on letters such as *K*, the tails of letters such as *Y* and *J*. What the professional handwriting examiner looks at and what the amateur hoping to identify handwriting looks at are often totally different; therefore, what an amateur may think is an exact replica of someone else's signature may, to a handwriting examiner, betray dozens of major points of difference.

Often a person will hope to disguise his/her handwriting by writing with the nonpreferred hand; that is, a left-handed person will write with the right hand. Although the writing to the untrained eye may look totally unlike the person's usual writing, the handwriting examiner can usually identify this writing easily by looking for brain-linked habits that transcend handedness.

When a questioned signature is *absolutely* identical with a known signature, it is likely to be a tracing, which can almost always be identified microscopically by the types of hesitations that do not occur in fluent natural handwriting.

For more information on handwriting identification, check the books in the bibliography. Your library should have many more; the subject is often addressed, and there are few major changes in the field. *The Hand of Hauptmann* is a fine book, which tells how handwriting identification helped to lead to the conviction of the kidnapper of the Lindbergh baby.

Printing and Typewriting

This is where we are regressing. Fifty years ago, a typewriter was a typewriter was a typewriter. It sat on a desk or was carried about, if it happened to be a portable. It had keys. The keys were interchangeable only by a technician, and even the technician had to work at it. Document examiners maintained data bases of type-faces and type sizes of different makes and models of typewriters, and as the typewriters aged, the type wore and got out of line. Furthermore, even with a new typewriter, the way the keys were hit had a lot to do with how good the typing looked.

Therefore, it was quite easy to look at the ransom note or the poison-pen letter and say, "This was typed on a five-year-old Royal 440 by an unskilled typist." And furthermore, when the typewriter was found, it could be definitely identified, and when various suspects were forced to type on that typewriter, there would be considerable likelihood of determining which suspect produced that vilely typed note.

But now we have typewriters and dedicated word processors and computers with interchangeable type fonts of all types and sizes, from type balls to Daisy wheels to laser printers. A letter typed on an IBM Correcting Selectric II by an unskilled typist doing hunt-and-peck isn't going to look much different from a letter typed on that same machine by a highly skilled typist, and if the type ball is dropped in the river three minutes after the letter is typed, the chances for identification—unless the investigator can get lucky enough to find some other materials typed by the suspect with the same somewhat-worn type ball—are zip.

That gives you something to play with.

Of course, handwriting and typewriting are not the only things involved with document examination; there are questions about inks, papers, watermarks, and so forth. But inks and papers are examined the same way other trace evidence is examined: with chromatography and other laboratory microscopic and radiometric devices. The problem comes when a good forger—one of the Mark Hofmann caliber—uses authentic paper of the appropriate age, makes ink by the formula appropriate to the purported document, and uses appropriate typefaces. It's not always possible to detect artificial aging.

Where do you go from there? (Read Jonathan Gash's mysteries for delightful insides on how fake antiques are created and artificially aged.)

Watch the news very carefully. While this book was being prepared for the press, a startling new development in crime-scene work was first used in court. It is a computer program that allows investigators to reconstruct, on the basis of what they have learned from both eyewitness testimony and crime-scene investigation, what happened each fraction of a second as the crime was occurring. It creates a timed, moving crime-scene sketch. Setting up the program is time-consuming and costly, but once it is set up, the program can actually rotate the scene so that it can be viewed from several different points of view, and can rearrange the situation when eyewitness testimonies differ so that the scene can be viewed as each eyewitness saw it, letting the jury determine what is most likely to have occurred. If the testimony of one eyewitness is impossible according to the physical evidence, the program will make that clear; if the testimonies of several eyewitnesses vary, but each — according to the physical evidence — is possible, that also will be clear.

Besides checking the feasibility of each witness's story, the program also allows the action to stop in a freeze-frame whenever the witness needs to explain something more fully, or the jury wants to consider what might have happened in that particular tenth of a second.

As this book goes to press, the program is available from only one company, and has been used in court only one time. But by the time the book is in the reader's hands, almost certainly similar programs — even more sophisticated ones — will be available in many places. This tool, even more than most tools of crime-scene investigation, can be used by both the prosecution and the defense.

The laboratory can do a lot of things. Individually, each one is only circumstantial. But how do they all add up?

A Prototype Case

Let's imagine a robbery and rape-murder.

The victim, glamorous starlet Brigette Garbo, has been found dead in her palatial ski condo in Ski City, Utah. She is wearing a white silk bra and a turquoise mohair sweater; nearby on the floor, apparently ripped off her, are a pair of white silk panties embroidered with pink-and-turquoise nylon thread and a pair of turquoise-

and-white wool slacks. Her body, lying on a sofa upholstered in a blue-and-beige, linen-and-cotton fabric, is covered with a fabulously expensive original Navajo blanket woven from natural, undyed, black, brown, and off-white wool. Fibers found on the body that did not come from anything in her condo include a light-blue dyed cotton and a white cotton-acrylic blend. Her hair, naturally black, has been bleached white and then dyed a sort of champagne blond; her pubic hair is still black. Tangled with her pubic hair, discovered by means of combings, are several brown pubic hairs, and one light-brown hair, about five inches long, is clinging to her mohair sweater. Alas, DNA fingerprinting is impossible; the perp seems to be aware of such things, as he apparently used a condom and took it with him, and none of the foreign hairs include the hair root.

Suspicion soon centers on condo handyman Ralph Kallikak, who was seen leaving her condo at three o'clock the afternoon of the crime. He insists he was there to change a faucet washer, and presents as evidence the fact that Brigette had called the condo office to report a leaking faucet, which is no longer leaking. But Ralph was throwing money around somewhat freely later in the afternoon, and Brigette's fabulous diamond tennis bracelet has turned up in a pawnshop, left there by a man who meets Ralph's description — a man about 5'6" tall, blue eyes, light-brown hair worn in a ponytail.

Police obtain a search warrant. When they examine the dirty clothes on the floor in Ralph's room (he doesn't seem to believe in hampers), they find a pair of faded blue jeans and a sweatshirt made of a white cotton-and-acrylic blend. On the jeans, they find microscopic fibers of white silk, turquoise mohair, turquoise-dyed wool, white-dyed wool, brown natural wool, black natural wool, and off-white natural wool, as well as blue-and-beige fibers of a mixture of cotton and linen. On the sweatshirt is one long hair, originally black but bleached white and dyed champagne blond. On his undershorts (yuck!) are a couple of black pubic hairs, but his own pubic hair is brown. Would you want to be Ralph's defense attorney?

The police reports and lab reports from this case are in the appendix.

TABLE 9
Sex-Crimes Evidence Collection

These pages come from the Evidence Collection Manual, *published by Sirchie Finger Print Laboratories, Inc., and are used by permission. The charts have been edited for use in this publication.*

Sexual assaults usually result in a physical struggle between the victim and the assailant. As a result of this struggle and the nature of sex crimes, physical evidence in some form is available to the investigator.

- Consider what types of evidence might be available as a result of the struggle — at the crime scene, on the victim, and on her clothing.
- Consider the type of weapon (if any) used in the commission of the assault.
- Consider how the assailant and the victim reached the crime scene.

Collection and Preservation

When Possible, Bloodstained Materials Should Be Sent to the Lab for Analysis

- Air dry the bloodstained material.
- Place the suspect material in a *paper* bag, affix an Evidence Collection Label, and mark with the date, your initials and an exhibit number. Seal the bag with an appropriate Evidence Integrity medium.
- Each bloodstained item must be packaged separately and *only after it is thoroughly air dried*.
- Collect standards for comparison.

When Bloodstained Materials Cannot Be Sent to the Lab For Analysis

- Using a clean blade, scrape the dried blood onto a clean piece of paper.
- Scrape the area immediately around the bloodstain onto another clean piece of paper.

- Fold and place each paper into the appropriate Rape Kit envelope.
- Initial, date, and assign exhibit numbers to all envelopes, and seal.
- Preserve and package the blade.
- Collect standards for comparison.

When a Sufficient Quantity of Liquid Blood is Available

- Fill vacutainer with blood.
- Initial, date, and assign an exhibit number to the vacutainer.

When a Whole Blood Sample Is not Available

- Using a gauze pad, soak up the moist blood.
- Air dry the pad.
- Place the pad in the appropriate Rape Kit Evidence Envelope; initial, date, and assign an exhibit number.
- Collect standards for comparison.

Collecting Blood Standards for Comparison

- Have a qualified individual collect whole blood from the victim and all suspects.
- Label vacutainers with all pertinent information.

DNA Analysis

The possibility of confirming an individual's identity by DNA *matching* makes the collection of physiological evidence imperative. To assist in the proper collection of liquid or whole blood samples for DNA matching, Sirchie Labs is placing in each of its Sex Crimes Evidence Collection Kits, a lavender topped vacutainer marked "DNA Blood Testing Sample" containing EDTA.

Collecting Saliva Samples

- Air dry the saliva-stained material on a piece of paper.
- Place the suspect material in a *paper* bag, affix an Evidence Collection label and mark with the date, your initials and an exhibit number. Seal the bag with an appropriate Evidence Integrity medium.
- Each saliva-stained item must be packaged separately, and only after it is *thoroughly* air dried.

- Collect standards for comparison.

Collecting Saliva Standards for Comparison

- Have the victim and the suspect(s) swab the inside of the mouth with the cotton swabs provided in the Rape Kit. Air dry and place in the appropriate envelope.
- Initial, date, and assign exhibit numbers to all envelopes, and seal.

Collecting Semen Samples

- Air dry the semen-stained material on a clean piece of paper.
- Place the suspect material in a *paper* bag, affix an Evidence Collection Label, and mark with the date, your initials and an exhibit number. Seal the bag with an appropriate Evidence Integrity medium.
- Each semen-stained item must be packaged separately, and only after it is *thoroughly* air dried.

T E N

THE UNOFFICIAL INVESTIGATOR

In every case . . . the Investigating Officer has first to obtain facts, often not without worry and trouble. As adversaries he has the accused, and often the witnesses, circumstances, natural events, difficulties that crop up from time to time. . . .

—Hans Gross,
Criminal Investigation

Throughout this book, I've been writing as if your fictional detective will be a police officer. Of course I realize that may not be true; s/he may be a private investigator, or a brilliant amateur. Nevertheless, most of this information remains useful. What can and cannot be determined by examining evidence, as well as how a crime scene and its evidence should be handled, remain the same.

But the unofficial investigator faces many problems that the police officer does not. To start with, simply gaining access to the evidence may be impossible. If the evidence has already been seized by the police, a court order — called a *motion for discovery*, obtainable by the defense attorney but not by the P.I. personally — may be required for the P.I. even to find out what evidence has been collected. The police, if they have not already been told by the prosecuting attorney not to, may decide to allow the P.I. to see the evidence, or they may not. (My usual practice, if I had no instructions from the D.A., was to allow the defense attorney to see the evidence only if it was so conclusive I felt my showing it would lead to a guilty plea.)

The P.I. certainly will not be allowed to take custody of the evidence, and lengthy court maneuvering might be required before the defense can get access to the evidence for an independent expert to examine it. If the court rules otherwise, the defense will never get access. Period.

The P.I. cannot, by law, get a search warrant, but if s/he enters illegally s/he may be charged with unlawful entry, burglary, or interfering with a police officer in the lawful discharge of his or her duty.

At the very best, even if the police and the witnesses all decide to cooperate with the P.I., the fact remains that the scene has been thoroughly worked over before the P.I. gets access to it. The P.I. will almost never have the advantage of seeing an undisturbed scene; therefore, s/he must almost always work with, through, or around someone else's interpretation of the scene.

And that "very best" situation rarely occurs. Usually the police will not cooperate, and the likelihood of a defense attorney's being hired and getting a court order requiring the P.I. to have access before the police are through working the scene is virtually nil—no matter how wealthy and well connected the suspect's family may be.

For an idea of the difficulty involved, consider the Sam Sheppard murder case: It took years, well after the defendant's conviction, for the defense to gain access to most of the evidence.

In addition to unavailable evidence and an already-worked-over scene, the P.I. may have another problem. Although police cannot actually compel possible witnesses to talk with them, they still carry some official clout, which the P.I does not have. If the P.I. is working for the defense, the prosecuting attorney may order possible witnesses not to talk; even without an order, a hostile witness who might feel compelled to talk with police—even if s/he is lying—may easily refuse to talk with any other investigators.

In real life, P.I.'s are rarely involved in murders; more often they are working with domestic matters or with corporate crime, where legal clout may be replaced with other types of clout. But in fiction, almost always the P.I. is working with murder or with something that may turn into murder.

One way to handle these problems is the way Rex Stout's detectives (other than Nero Wolfe, who almost never left his house) worked it. Think about how many times Archie or Stout's other detectives somehow managed to be first on the scene of the murder.

But even the most handy device can be used to excess. For an idea of what would happen in real life, let's look again at the murder of Brigette Garbo from the previous chapter. Let's suppose that Brigette's agent, Sam Snoop, who was hopelessly in love with her, has the idea that it was Brigette's husband-before-last, Peter Prowler, who killed her, and framed poor Ralph for the crime. So he calls you in—P.I. Anny Boddy. What are you going to do?

You're going to tread carefully, because, buddy, that California license doesn't mean Jack in Utah. You have no authority at all, legal or otherwise.

The first thing you want is access to the scene, and that's your first hurdle, when you find out that Brigette was still married to Peter Prowler when she bought the condo, and it was joint property. So now Peter owns it, and is he going to let you inside?

Scratch that.

So you go down to the Ski City Police Department and ask to speak to the investigating officer, Molly Murphy. Molly is in charge of the sex-crimes unit, and she has no time to talk to you, and anyway, she disapproves of Sam Snoop for very good reasons of her own which she sees no reason to discuss with you. What does that mean?

It means you aren't going to get a look at any of the crime-scene photographs or any of the evidence.

But wait a minute. If Snoop wants to convict somebody else, that means he's sort of on Ralph's side, because he doesn't want Ralph to get convicted, so you go and talk to Ralph's lawyer.

Who is Ralph's lawyer?

He's a public defender, of course, because since when could a maintenance man afford an attorney?

He's a public defender, which means he probably graduated from law school last year, and although he knows quite well what a motion for discovery is, he's never filed one in real life, and the idea makes his stomach hurt. He can get the format from a book, but he's not very happy about trying to follow the format, and he's not 100 percent sure it will work.

Well, that's okay; Sam Snoop can afford to hire a more expensive lawyer. You get a motion for discovery.

That means the district attorney has to tell you what evidence there is against Ralph. It does not mean Molly has to talk to you. It does not mean the State Crime Laboratory or the State Medical Examiner's Office, both located in Salt Lake City, have to give you any information. It does not mean you can get an independent expert to look at the evidence.

While the lawyers have been playing their legal games, you haven't been sitting still. No, you've been out to the condo, where you find there's been a sudden meeting of the condo owners association and guess what? It's embarrassing enough that Brigette was murdered there and Ralph has been arrested. Do you think anybody is going to talk to you?

If you do, think again.

At this point, you have exhausted all of the usual places for beginning an investigation, and for all practical purposes you haven't begun your investigation at all.

Does this mean P.I.'s—in real life or fiction—can't function?

No. It does mean that P.I.'s have to be smart. In real life, smart is enough. In fiction, the P.I. had better be very, very smart.

Of course, there are ways around many of these problems. Many fictional P.I.'s have close friends on the police department who will leak them information, or close friends who are crime reporters and will let them in on the little secrets that the police asked them not to print.

Many other fictional P.I.'s work almost entirely on the basis of the psychological elements of the crime and the talking-to-people area of investigation, and avoid crime scenes most of the time.

And in fiction, unlike real life, the P.I. sometimes is the first person on the scene of the murder.

You know what s/he *should* do then—back off, call the police, and stay out of the way. But if you read enough fiction to have any business thinking about writing it, you also know what s/he *will* do— surreptitiously search the victim's pockets if that seems called for; collect part of the evidence if possible (surely the police don't need *all* of this cup of probably poisoned coffee); examine the evidence if collecting it would be too damning (don't mess with the brass ejected by the automatic, but if you look at it long enough to find out the caliber and make, well, the police won't know the difference); sketch the scene; maybe take a photo or two; and then call the police.

In real life, this would certainly lose you your license; it might also lead to an arrest for murder or for accessory after the fact. But in fiction it works well.

This is the state of crime-scene investigation today. It has been said that writing is one part inspiration and nine parts perspiration. Crime-scene work is the same. The nine parts perspiration are critical; if the evidence isn't treated right, it can't tell anybody anything. But that one part inspiration is equally critical. It's the matter of knowing what to ask the evidence.

I Know Who Did It But I Can't Prove It

Sometimes it's maddening — situations in which police know who did it and know there is no way they can possibly prove it to the jury. I remember one case, a burglary, that I went to with Doc, after I'd been on the department about eighteen months. On the way back into the police station, I said, "Doc, that didn't look right."

"What didn't look right?" he asked.

"The whole thing," I said. "It didn't look like a burglary. It looked like the stage setting for act two, scene one, the crime is discovered."

Doc chuckled. "And now," he said, "you can call yourself a crime-scene officer."

Why Is an Innocent Person on Trial?

And sometimes, if you're an expert, you know that somebody who is commonly believed guilty is innocent. Several years after I left police work, I read about a case like that. An industrialist had been accused of setting up the murder-for-hire of a judge. The proposed assassin had reported to police, and police and the judge had worked together. The assassin told his employer the job was done, and the police moved in. The employer was charged not with murder, because the judge was perfectly healthy, but with conspiracy.

The newspapers were carrying blow-by-blow accounts of the trial, and I was interested. Several times people who knew my background asked me what I thought, and each time I replied, "I didn't work the case." At that point, neither the prosecution nor the defense had made a case, as far as I was concerned.

And then along came a crucial bit of testimony. The "murderer" had taken a Polaroid picture of the judge, supposedly dead, in the trunk of a car. (The judge had cooperated by climbing into the trunk and posing for the picture.) Police then coated the picture with thief detection powder, and the "murderer" supposedly showed the picture to his employer, who handled it, examined it closely, and returned it—inside a white Cadillac. When the employer was arrested within the next two hours, there was no trace of thief detection powder on his clothing, his person, or his car upholstery. And that was the point at which I said, "This man is innocent."

Why?

Because I've worked with thief detection powder. It is almost invisible when it's dry; in fact, when it's dry and spread thin you need ultraviolet light to see it. But it clings—oh, how it clings! You cannot brush it off—any attempt to do so merely spreads it. You cannot wash it off. The more you wash, the more purple your hands and clothing become.

The day somebody spilled some thief detection powder and I accidentally sat in it, I wound up having to completely discard the clothing I was wearing; ten washings with strong detergents and bleach did not wash the stuff out, and despite washing with every kind of soap I could think of, my hands did not get clean. It took about a week for the stuff to wear off.

And the prosecution team was trying to make a jury believe that this man handled a photograph liberally coated with this powder, but had no trace of it left two hours later? That's not even a good joke.

The jury agreed.

The work continues. As I took a break from this chapter long enough to watch the television news, I saw clips of a blood-spatter expert from California entering a West Valley, Utah, house, where two weeks ago, a woman and three children were knifed to death. Police think they know who did it, but they can't prove it. They hope the blood-spatter expert will help them prove it.

Right now I don't have an opinion. I didn't work the case. But I'll be interested in watching it develop.

This has been an overview of the state of crime-scene investigation today. I strongly recommend that you locate and read as many as possible of the books in my bibliography and other books like them, and that you keep constantly informed on changes. This is one of the fields, like physics and astronomy, in which what is true today and what is true tomorrow may not be the same thing. It was exciting to work in; it is exciting to read about and to write about.

And there's one important difference between real crime and fictional crime. In real life, people love to kill each other at two o'clock in the morning.

You don't have to write at 2:00 A.M. unless you want to.

But, weirdos that we are, most of us want to.

TABLE 10
What Is That Thing?

When you know what something looks like but not what it's called —
or you know where on some other object it's located but not what
it's called — or you know from other research what it's called but
you're a little vague about exactly what it is or what it does — special
reference books might help you.

The Facts on File Visual Dictionary enables you — as it says on
the cover — to "look up the word from the picture and the picture
from the word." It's well organized and extremely easy to use, and
I consult it often.

A good encyclopedia, particularly one such as *World Book* that
is designed largely for children's use, tends to be very well illustrated, with fine drawings and exploded diagrams. If at all possible,
you should have at least one encyclopedia in your home. Often out-
of-date encyclopedias, which for most purposes other than history,
geography, politics, astronomy and physics are entirely adequate,
are available from library sales or used bookstores for as little as
twenty-five dollars a set.

As words change so much, and so many new words enter the
language every year, there's really no substitute for purchasing a
new dictionary at least every ten years. For most purposes, the most
recent *Merriam-Webster College Dictionary* is adequate; when you
need an unabridged, which is outside the price range of most of us,
you can always make a trip to the library.

Any mystery or true crime writer should own at least one book
on human anatomy. *Gray's Anatomy*, originally published in 1901,
was republished by Crown in 1977 in a beautifully illustrated edition.
It remains the classic in the field, and is generally available, particularly by mail order, at a reasonable cost. Any other good anatomy,
such as Helen Dawson's *Basic Human Anatomy*, is acceptable, although most of them are not as well illustrated as Gray's.

I really haven't found any satisfactory substitute for *Taber's
Cyclopedic Medical Dictionary*, which helps to clarify matters on
which other medical forensic books are unclear.

Dictionaries of criminal slang may be very useful, but bear in
mind that slang becomes dated quickly. This means that it is critical

to use a slang dictionary written during, or historically written about, the exact period and area the writer has in mind.

A thesaurus can help the writer to locate a word conveying the exact shade of meaning s/he has in mind. A dictionary-style thesaurus, which enables you to look up a specific word and then look for related words, is usually easier to use than a topical thesaurus, but you may find you prefer the topical style. Either is excellent.

Afterword

I do not subscribe to the tenet that everything that is worth doing is worth doing well. Bed making, for example, should in my opinion be done as quickly and as seldom as possible, and when someone is writing a book, s/he may be excused for not sweeping the floor until the dust-bunnies start chasing the cats.

But every book that you write, published or not, is likely to outlive you. A published book will certainly outlive its author.

I keep thinking of a book I once read in which the author proclaimed that all the houses in Texas look alike (they range from mansion to shanty; tar paper siding to wood siding to asbestos siding to aluminum siding to brick to stone; wood frame to steel frame to adobe); that orange trees grow in Tyler, Texas (the closest to Tyler you'll find orange trees is the Corpus Christi area, almost a full day's drive to the south); and that the landing approach to a particular airport is over barren mud flats (when I flew into that airport, the approach was over a lush pine forest).

We can all make mistakes, and I make my full share of them. But there is absolutely no excuse for egregious laziness in writing. The information is available, and we have the responsibility to make our fiction as truthful in factual areas as we possibly can.

The fact that you're reading this book proves that you care. I hope I've helped you to meet your goals.

Appendix A

Initial Crime Report

Anytown Police Department   **Case Number:** 91-12-0056

Offense: Rape/Homicide
Victim: Brigette Garbo W/F   **DOB:** 2-14-61
Location: 809 Pine Valley Road #12, living room
Date: Tuesday Dec. 9, 1991   **Time:** around 1500 hrs.
Means: apparently manual strangulation
Weapon: hands
Details:

Reporting officer arrived at 809 Pine Valley Road, Condo Number 12, at 1615 hrs., in response to a reported homicide. Complainant Valerie Valdosta stated she works in office, had sent Ralph Kallikak to vict.'s condo about 1500 hrs. to fix leaky faucet, had tried later to call vict. to see if work was done. Getting no answer, she went to vict.'s apartment and could see body through front window. Complainant then returned to office and called police and then met us at Condo 12 with the master key.

R/o stayed at scene and awaited arrival of detectives. Case was then turned over to Detective Molly Murphy. On orders of Detective Murphy, R/o remained at door to protect scene from intruders.

Rick Tracy, PH.

Appendix B

Supplemental Report

Anytown Police Department   **Case Number:** 91-12-0056

On December 9, 1991, I went to 809 Pine Valley Road, Condo 12, in response to a request by Officer Tracy for detectives to work a reported homicide. Victim, identified to me by Valerie Valdosta as Brigette Garbo, was in front room lying on couch. The body was lying on its left side, facing north, with the top of the head pointing west, partially covered with black, brown, and off-white Indian blanket. Body was wearing turquoise sweater pulled up to expose part of white bra.

On the floor north of the couch was a pair of turquoise-and-white slacks and a pair of white panties with pink-and-turquoise embroidery. Both were ripped slightly at the front of the waistband, and the panties were still inside the slacks.

I directed Crime Scene Technician Anny Boddy to make a full investigation. I then went to get a statement from Valerie Valdosta. (See statement.) Ms. Valdosta told me that Ralph Kallikak, who had been sent about 1500 hrs. to fix leaky faucet at victim's condo, was now missing.

I later returned to scene to assist Anny Boddy in measurements. After body was released, I accompanied body to hospital. At hospital, I observed pathologist Dr. Kuttim Up as he used rape kit and turned it over to me. I collected the following items of evidence:

91-12-0056-M1: turquoise sweater from victim's body
91-12-0056-M2: white bra from victim's body
91-12-0056-M3: combings from victim's pubic hair
91-12-0056-M4: washings from victim's vagina
91-12-0056-M5: scrapings from under victim's fingernails, right hand
91-12-0056-M6: scrapings from under victim's fingernails, left hand
91-12-0056-M7: combings from victim's hair, right front
91-12-0056-M8: combings from victim's hair, left front

91-12-0056-M9: combings from victim's hair, right rear
91-12-0056-M10: combings from victim's hair, left rear

At that point, Anny Boddy arrived from the scene, to attempt to get perp's fingerprints from victim's abdominal, breast, thigh, and inner arms. See Off. Boddy's report.

I turned the evidence I had collected over to Off. Boddy and returned to scene to see if Mr. Kallikak had returned. He had not.

Additional report will follow.

Det. Molly Murphy
Dec. 9, 1991

Appendix C

Supplemental Crime Report

Anytown Police Department   **Case Number:** 91-12-0056

    This officer was called to 809 Pine Valley Road, Condo 12, in response to a request by Det. Molly Murphy for a full crime-scene investigation. Det. Murphy told me the victim, Brigette Garbo, was in front room. She led me to the body of a white female, about thirty years old, lying partly on its left side on a blue-and-beige smooth-upholstered couch. Victim was facing north, with the top of her head pointing west. Top of head was ten feet five inches south of the north wall and thirteen feet nine inches west of the east wall. Her body was twisted at the waist, so that the lower part of the body was on its back with legs parted. Victim was wearing turquoise sweater pulled up to expose part of white bra. Victim was partially covered with brown, black, and off-white Indian-style blanket.

    On the floor north of the couch, six-and-a-half feet south of the north wall and fourteen feet three inches west of the east wall, was a pair of turquoise-and-white slacks and a pair of white panties with pink-and-turquoise embroidery. Both were ripped slightly at the front of the waistband, and the panties were still inside the slacks.

    After getting this information, I searched the entire scene. There was no evidence of disturbance in any other room. There was no sign of forcible entry.

    With the aid of Det. Murphy, who had returned to the scene, I made complete measurements and made a sketch of the living room.

    The following items of evidence were then collected:
91-12-0056-1: turquoise-and-white slacks from floor
91-12-0056-2: white panties from floor
91-12-0056-3: brown, black, and off-white Indian blanket
Body was then released. Det. Murphy accompanied body to hospital.

    Using evidence vacuum, I collected the following additional evidence:

91-12-0056-4: sweepings from northernmost cushion on couch

91-12-0056-5: sweepings from middle cushion on couch

91-12-0056-6: sweepings from southernmost cushion on couch

91-12-0056-7: sweepings from under and behind northernmost cushion on couch

91-12-0056-8: sweepings from under and behind middle cushion on couch

91-12-0056-9: sweepings from under and behind southernmost cushion on couch

I then dusted for fingerprints in the following areas, with the following results:

polished wooden floor in living room—no usable prints developed

kitchen—no usable prints developed. Water marks indicated that countertops, metal faucets and appliance surfaces had been recently wiped down

bathroom—no usable prints developed. Water marks indicated that countertops and metal faucets had been recently wiped down. Due to possibility of robbery, no investigation has yet been made in bedroom. Uniform officers will keep area under guard until victim's agent, who knows her possessions well, arrives from California to check.

I then went to hospital, where I tried for fingerprints on victim's skin. No prints were developed.

Det. Murphy turned the following evidence over to me:

91-12-0056-M1: turquoise sweater from victim's body

91-12-0056-M2: white bra from victim's body

91-12-0056-M3: combings from victim's pubic hair

91-12-0056-M4: washings from victim's vagina

91-12-0056-M5: scrapings from under victim's fingernails, right hand

91-12-0056-M6: scrapings from under victim's fingernails, left hand

91-12-0056-M7: combings from victim's hair, right front

91-12-0056-M8: combings from victim's hair, left front

91-12-0056-M9: combings from victim's hair, right rear

91-12-0056-M10: combings from victim's hair, left rear

At 1800 hrs., I went to apartment of suspect Ralph Kallikak under Det. Murphy's search warrant. At the direction of Det. Murphy, I collected the following additional items:

91-12-0056-10: white sweatshirt, size M, from bedroom floor

91-12-0056-11: Levi's brand denim jeans, size not visible, from bedroom floor

91-12-0056-12: Jockey brand undershorts, extremely stained and frayed, from bedroom floor

I then accompanied Det. Murphy to county jail, where suspect Ralph Kallikak was confined. Det. Murphy and I took suspect to county hospital, where physician's assistant Pat Patterson, acting on court order, took blood samples and pubic and head hair combing from suspect and turned them over to us. These were labeled as follows:

91-12-0056-13: blood sample from Ralph Kallikak

91-12-0056-14: pubic hair combings from Ralph Kallikak

91-12-0056-15: head hair combings from Ralph Kallikak, right front

91-12-0056-16: head hair combings from Ralph Kallikak, left front

91-12-0056-17: head hair combings from Ralph Kallikak, right rear

91-12-0056-18: head hair combings from Ralph Kallikak, left rear

I then locked evidence in evidence locker. I will transport it to state crime lab next date.

Supplemental reports will follow.

Onny Brodder, Ptl.

Dec. 9, 1991

Appendix D

Laboratory Report
State Crime Laboratory

TO: Investigator Anny Boddy
FROM: Clem Huddle, Ph.D.
DATE: January 4, 1992
RE: Your case # 91-12-0056

On December 10, 1991, you turned over to me in my office the following items, your identifying numbers:

91-12-0056-1: turquoise-and-white slacks from floor
91-12-0056-2: white panties from floor
91-12-0056-3: brown, black, and off-white Indian blanket
91-12-0056-4: sweepings from northernmost cushion on couch
91-12-0056-5: sweepings from middle cushion on couch
91-12-0056-6: sweepings from southernmost cushion on couch
91-12-0056-7: sweepings from under and behind northernmost cushion on couch
91-12-0056-8: sweepings from under and behind middle cushion on couch
91-12-0056-9: sweepings from under and behind southernmost cushion on couch
9l-12-0056-10: white sweatshirt, size M, from bedroom floor
91-12-0056-11: Levi's brand denim jeans, size not visible, from bedroom floor
91-12-0056-12: Jockey brand undershorts, extremely stained and frayed, from bedroom floor
91-12-0056-13: blood sample from Ralph Kallikak
91-12-0056-14: pubic hair combings from Ralph Kallikak
91-12-0056-15: head hair combings from Ralph Kallikak, right front
91-12-0056-16: head hair combings from Ralph Kallikak, left front
91-12-0056-17: head hair combings from Ralph Kallikak, right rear

91-12-0056-18: head hair combings from Ralph Kallikak, left rear

91-12-0056-M1: turquoise sweater from victim's body

91-12-0056-M2: white bra from victim's body

91-12-0056-M3: combings from victim's pubic hair

91-12-0056-M4: washings from victim's vagina

91-12-0056-M5: scrapings from under victim's fingernails, right hand

91-12-0056-M6: scrapings from under victim's fingernails, left hand

91-12-0056-M7: combings from victim's hair, right front

91-12-0056-M8: combings from victim's hair, left front

91-12-0056-M9: combings from victim's hair, right rear

91-12-0056-M10: combings from victim's hair, left rear

Examinations were made, and the following results were obtained:

91-12-0056-1: turquoise-and-white slacks from floor. Slacks are dyed wool. Numerous fibers of turquoise-dyed mohair, which could have come from your item 91-12-0056-M1, were found clinging to surface. Numerous fibers of blue-and-beige dyed cotton-linen mix, which could have come from the same source as your items 91-12-0056-4 through 91-0056-9 inclusive, were found clinging to surface. Numerous fibers of black, brown, and off-white undyed wool, which could have come from your item 91-12-0056-3, were found clinging.

91-12-0056-2: white panties from floor. Panties are silk with pink-and-turquoise silk thread embroidery. Waistband has a rip 7 mm long at front. No foreign fibers were on it.

91-12-0056-3: brown, black, and off-white Indian blanket. Blanket has clinging to it numerous turquoise-dyed mohair and turquoise-and-white wool fibers which could have come from clothing identified as victim's.

91-12-0056-4: sweepings from northernmost cushion on couch. This cushion had clinging to it numerous fibers of brown, black, and off-white undyed wool that could have come from your item 91-12-0056-3 and hairs that matched most hairs from victim's combings, your numbers 91-12-0056-M7 through 91-12-0056-M10 inclusive.

91-12-0056-5: sweepings from the middle cushion on

couch. This cushion had clinging to it numerous fibers of brown, black, and off-white undyed wool, which could have come from your item 91-12-0056-3 and hairs that matched most hairs from victim's combings, your numbers 91-12-0056-M7 through 91-12-0056-M10 inclusive. Also clinging to it were fibers of turquoise-and-white wool fibers, which could have come from clothing identified as victim's.

91-12-0056-6: sweepings from southernmost cushion on couch. No foreign fibers were found in these sweepings.

91-12-0056-7: sweepings from under and behind northernmost cushion on couch. These sweepings contained numerous foreign particles (see supplemental report), which did not match any of your samples. Sweepings also contained small amounts of marijuana and cocaine.

91-12-0056-8: sweepings from under and behind middle cushion on couch. These sweepings contained numerous foreign particles (see supplemental report), which did not match any of your samples. Sweepings also contained small amounts of marijuana and cocaine.

91-12-0056-9: sweepings from under and behind southernmost cushion on couch. These sweepings contained numerous foreign particles (see supplemental report), which did not match any of your samples. Sweepings also contained small amounts of marijuana and cocaine.

91-12-0056-10: white sweatshirt, size M, from bedroom floor. One hair was clinging to front right shoulder. Hair appeared to be black, bleached, and then dyed blond. Hair was identical in all characteristics to majority of hair found in combings your numbers 91-12-0056-M7 through 91-12-0056-M10 inclusive.

91-12-0056-11: Levi's brand denim jeans, size not visible, from bedroom floor. Clinging to jeans were fibers of undyed wool, black, brown, and off-white, similar in all characteristics to the wool comprising your item 91-12-0056-3.

91-12-0056-12: Jockey brand undershorts, extremely stained and frayed, from bedroom floor. Clinging to interior front of shorts were 12 brown pubic hairs matching your item 91-12-0056-14: pubic hair combings from Ralph Kallikak and two black pubic hairs similar to your item 91-12-0056-M3: combings from victim's pubic hair.

91-12-0056-13: blood sample from Ralph Kallikak. Blood is type B, Rhesus positive. Subject is suffering from syphilis and should be isolated from general jail population and placed in treatment at once.

91-12-0056-14: pubic hair combings from Ralph Kallikak. Combings are clean and contain no foreign matter.

91-12-0056-15: head hair combings from Ralph Kallikak, right front. Combings are clean and contain no foreign matter.

91-12-0056-16: head hair combings from Ralph Kallikak, left front. Combings are clean and contain no foreign matter.

91-12-0056-17: head hair combings from Ralph Kallikak, right rear. Combings are clean and contain no foreign matter.

91-12-0056-18: head hair combings from Ralph Kallikak, left rear. Combings are clean and contain no foreign matter.

91-12-0056-M1: turquoise sweater from victim's body. Sweater is made of turquoise-dyed mohair. One brown hair, five inches in length, was clinging to it. Hair matches in all characteristics your sample 91-12-0056-15 through 91-12-0056-18.

91-12-0056-M2: white bra from victim's body. Bra is white silk. Turquoise-dyed fibers clinging to it match in all characteristics fibers from your 91-12-0056-M1.

91-12-0056-M3: combings from victim's pubic hair. Most combings are black in color. Two short brown hairs found in combings match in all characteristics your sample 91-12-0056-14.

91-12-0056-M4: washings from victim's vagina. Washings contain blood, which matches blood of victim, submitted by your medical examiner. No semen is present. No foreign blood is present.

91-12-0056-M5: scrapings from under victim's fingernails, right hand. Contents include three small fibers of blue-dyed cotton, which could have come from your item 91-12-0056-11.

91-12-0056-M6: scrapings from under victim's fingernails, left hand. No foreign material found.

91-12-0056-M7: combings from victim's hair, right front. Hair was originally black, was bleached out and then dyed a color called Champagne Blonde, Brand XYZ. No foreign material detected.

91-12-0056-M8: combings from victim's hair, left front. Hair was originally black, was bleached out and then dyed a color called Champagne Blonde, Brand XYZ. No foreign material detected.

91-12-0056-M9: combings from victim's hair, right rear. Hair was originally black, was bleached out and then dyed a color called Champagne Blonde, Brand XYZ. No foreign material detected.

91-12-0056-M10: combings from victim's hair, left rear. Hair was originally black, was bleached out and then dyed a color called Champagne Blonde, Brand XYZ. No foreign material detected.

Per your request, items are retained in laboratory until court date is set.

Clem Huddle, Ph.D.

aphy

ior. *Identification System for Questioned Documents*. Springfield, Ill.: 1970.

Bates, ___ Prior. *Typewriting Identification: (I.S.Q.T.) Identification System for Questioned Typewriting*. Springfield, Ill.: Thomas, 1971.

Block, Eugene. *Hypnosis: A New Tool in Crime Detection*. New York: McKay, 1976.

Burrard, Gerald. *The Identification of Firearms and Forensic Ballistics*. New York: Barnes, 1962.

Burroway, Janet. *Writing Fiction: A Guide to Narrative Craft*. Boston: Little, Brown and Co., 1987.

Committee on Evaluation of Sound Spectrograms, Assembly of Behavioral and Social Sciences, National Research Council. *On the Theory and Practice of Voice Identification*. Washington, D.C.: National Academy of Sciences, 1979.

Conway, James V.P. *Evidential Documents*. Springfield, Ill.: Thomas, 1959.

Cormack, A.J.R. *Famous Rifles and Machine Guns*. Windsor, Eng.: Profile, 1977.

Davies, Geoffrey, ed. *Forensic Science*. 2d ed. Washington, D.C.: American Chemical Society, 1986.

Eckert, William G., and Stuart H. James. *Interpretation of Bloodstain Evidence at Crime Scenes*. New York: Elsevier, 1989.

Fallis, Greg, and Ruth Greenberg. *Be Your Own Detective*. New York: M. Evans and Co., 1989.

Field, Annita T. *Fingerprint Handbook*. Springfield, Ill.: Thomas, 1976.

Gaute, J.H.H., and Robin Odell. *The Murderers' Who's Who*. London: Methuen Publishing Co., 1979.

Gerasimov, Mikhail Mikhailovich. *The Face Finder*. tr. Alan Houghton Brodrick. London: Hutchinson, 1971.

Gonzales, Thomas et al. *Legal Medicine: Pathology and Toxicology*. New York: Appleton, 1954.

Gross, Hans. *Criminal Investigation: A Practical Textbook for Magistrates, Police Officers and Lawyers*. London: Sweet & Maxwell, Ltd., 1934.

Hall, Jay Cameron. *Inside the Crime Lab*. Englewood Cliffs, N.J.: Prentice-Hall, 1974.

Hardy, Richard E., and John G. Cull. *Drug Language and Lore*. Springfield, Ill.: Thomas, 1975.

Haring, J. Vreeland. *The Hand of Hauptmann*. Plainfield, N.J.: Hamer, 1937.

Hicks, Randolph D. *Undercover Operations and Persuasion*. Springfield, Ill.: Thomas, 1973.

Horne, Peter. *Women in Law Enforcement*. Springfield, Ill.: Thomas, 1975.

Joyce, Christopher, and Eric Stover. *Witnesses from the Grave: The Stories Bones Tell*. Boston: Little, Brown and Co., 1991.

Kevorkian, Jack. *Prescription—Medicide: The Goodness of Planned Death*. Buffalo, N.Y.: Prometheus Books, 1991.

Kolata, Gina. "Gene Test Barred as Proof in Court." *New York Times*, 14 Feb. 1991.

McArdle, Phil, and Karen McArdle. *Fatal Fascination*. Boston: Houghton, 1988.

McGarvey, Robert, and Elise Caitlin. *The Complete Spy*. New York: Perigee, 1983.

Matunas, Edward. *American Ammunition and Ballistics*. Tulsa, Ariz.: Winchester, 1979.

Melling, John Kennedy. *The Crime Writers' Practical Handbook of Technical Information*. London: The Crime Writers' Association, 1989.

Miller, Jonathan. *The Body in Question*. New York: Random House, 1978.

Mullin, Timothy J. *Training the Gunfighter*. Boulder, Co.: Paladin Press, 1981.

National Institute of Justice. *Crime Scene Search and Physical Evidence Handbook*. Washington, D.C.: U.S. Department of Justice, 1973.

National Institute of Justice. *Forensic Evidence and the Police*. Washington, D.C.: U.S. Department of Justice, 1984.

Newton, Michael. *Armed and Dangerous: A Writer's Guide to Weapons*. Cincinnati: Writer's Digest Books, 1990.

Noguchi, Thomas T. *Coroner*. New York: Simon & Schuster, 1983.

Noguchi, Thomas T. with Joseph DiMona. *Coroner at Large*. New York: Simon & Schuster, 1985.

Olsen, Robert D. *Scott's Fingerprint Mechanics*. Springfield, Ill.: Thomas, 1978.

Queenan, Joe. "Skeleton Keys." *Wall Street Journal*, 12 Feb. 1991.

Rensberger, Boyce. "FBI Director Rebuts Critics of DNA Fingerprinting." *Salt Lake Tribune*, 26 Dec. 1991.

Roth, Martin. *The Writer's Complete Crime Reference Book*. Cincinnati: Writer's Digest Books, 1990.

Sayers, Dorothy L. "In the Teeth of the Evidence." In *In the Teeth of the Evidence*. 1940. Reprint. New York: Avon, 1967. 5-16.

Sirchie Finger Print Laboratories, Inc. *Evidence Collection Manual*. Raleigh, N.C.: Sirchie, 1991.

Sirchie Finger Print Laboratories, Inc. *The Finger Print Manual*. Raleigh, N.C.: Sirchie, 1991.

Steiner, Bradley J. *Below the Belt: Unarmed Combat for Women*. Boulder, Co.: Paladin Press, 1976.

Stevens, Serita Deborah, with Anne Klarner. *Deadly Doses: A Writer's Guide to Poisons*. Cincinnati: Writer's Digest Books, 1990.

Thorwald, Jurgen. *The Century of the Detective*. tr. Richard Winston and Clara Winston. New York: Harcourt, Brace & World, 1964.

Thorwald, Jurgen. *Crime and Science: The New Frontier in Criminology*. tr. Richard Winston and Clara Winston. New York: Harcourt, Brace & World, 1966.

Turner, William W. *Invisible Witness: The Use and Abuse of the New Technology of Crime Investigation*. New York: Bobbs-Merrill, 1968.

U.S. Department of Justice. *Automated Fingerprint Identification Systems: Technology and Policy Issues*. Washington, D.C.: U.S. Department of Justice, 1987.

U.S. Department of Justice. *Handbook of Forensic Science*. Washington, D.C.: U.S. Department of Justice, 1984.

Ubell, Earl. "Whodunit? Quick, Check the Genes!" *Parade* (3 Mar. 1991): 12ff.

Wagner, Diane. *Corpus Delicti: The True Story of L. Ewing Scott, Convicted of Murder Without a Confession or a Corpse*. New York: St. Martin's Press, 1986.

Watanabe, Tomio. *Atlas of Legal Medicine*. New York: Lippincott, 1975.

Wilson, Keith. *Cause of Death: A Writer's Guide to Death, Murder and Forensic Medicine*. Cincinnati: Writer's Digest Books, 1992.

Index